Burning Messages on All-Out Discipleship

WHAT IT COSTS TO BE A Good Christian

By

Evangelist John R. Rice, D.D., Litt.D.

Editor, *The Sword of the Lord*

SWORD OF THE LORD PUBLISHERS

Murfreesboro Tennessee

5,000 copies first printing, June, 1952
8,000 copies second printing, February, 1953
1,000 copies third printing, February, 1966
1,000 copies fourth printing, May, 1969
1,000 copies fifth printing, May, 1972
1,000 copies sixth printing, January, 1974
1,500 copies seventh printing. May, 1975
2,000 copies eighth printing, January, 1977

ISBN 0-87398-905-8

PRINTED IN U. S. A.

Author's Preface

MANY PEOPLE mistakenly suppose that an evangelist should simply preach to the unsaved and nothing but the plan of salvation. That is far from the truth, as the ministry of all the great evangelists proves. It is also unscriptural. In Ephesians 4:11, 12 Paul, by divine inspiration, says: "And he gave some, apostles; and some, prophets; and some, evangelists; and some, pastors and teachers; For the perfecting of the saints for the work of the ministry." Evangelists, then, are "for the perfecting of the saints for the work of the ministry." Evangelists are "for the edifying of the body of Christ." In other words, an evangelist is called of God to preach on discipleship and to make good Christians.

In over thirty years' ministry I have felt a continual urge from God to preach on the cost of discipleship. I have earnestly labored not only to make converts, but to make the converts into good Christians.

Now with deep burden of soul I send out these favorite messages on all-out discipleship. If we make good Christians, then we make happy Christians, soul-winning, powerful Christians. May God make us fit to follow in the train of prophets, apostles, martyrs, evangelists, and missionary heroes of the past, leaving all for Jesus.

JOHN R. RICE

June, 1952

HEAVEN'S AWARD OF MERIT

"Well done, good and faithful servant"!

These few words of commendation from the Saviour will be the most thrilling, satisfying, meaningful words you and I can ever hear. They will constitute Heaven's highest Award of Merit for those soldiers of the Cross who have courageously and conscientiously borne the Cross in the day of their earthly pilgrimage. There can be no higher honor to any Christian.

His word to us will be "Well done," *if,* after we have counted the cost of being His disciple, we have denied ourselves stedfastly and have sought first His glory; if we have obeyed Him implicitly wherever He has sent us; if we have trusted Him where we could not always trace Him; if we have run with patience the race set before us and have finished the course with joy.

We cannot be overcoming Christians without counting the cost, and then paying it to the full. In these pages God's servant tells us plainly and lovingly about that cost, and the glorious results that will be ours, both in time and in eternity, for paying the full cost.

It will be worth it all when we see the Lord Jesus!

V. R. EDMAN
Late President, Wheaton College
Wheaton, Illinois

Contents

Acknowledgments

"I Met God in the Morning" is from *Spiritual Hill Tops,* copyright 1932 by Ralph S. Cushman. Used by permission of Abingdon-Cokesbury Press.

"Read the Bible Through" and "The Bible," by Amos R. Wells, copyright by International Society of Christian Endeavor. Used by their permission.

What It Costs to Be a Good Christian

"And the king said unto Araunah, Nay; but I will surely buy it of thee at a price: neither will I offer burnt-offerings unto the Lord my God of that which doth cost me nothing."
—II Samuel 24:24.

WHEN DAVID was king in Israel, he grew vain and proud of his great kingdom and his mighty army. So he sent Joab, his general, to take a census of all the fighting men in his empire. This pride was a sin. It showed that David and his people were depending on their own might instead of on the protection of God. God made it an occasion of great punishment, and from Dan to Beer-sheba some seventy thousand men died of a pestilence. But when the angel of God stretched out his hand toward Jerusalem to destroy it, God in mercy intervened and the prophet Gad was sent to David. Now read the story in words of Scripture:

"And Gad came that day to David, and said unto him, Go up, rear an altar unto the Lord in the threshingfloor of Araunah the Jebusite. And David, according to the saying of Gad, went up as the Lord commanded. And Araunah looked, and saw the king and his servants coming on toward him: and Araunah went out, and bowed himself before the king on his face upon the ground. And Araunah said, Wherefore is my lord the king come to his servant? And David said, To

buy the threshingfloor of thee, to build an altar unto the Lord, that the plague may be stayed from the people. And Araunah said unto David, Let my lord the king take and offer up what seemeth good unto him: behold, here be oxen for burnt-sacrifice, and threshing instruments and other instruments of the oxen for wood. All these things did Araunah, as a king, give unto the king. And Araunah said unto the king, The Lord thy God accept thee. And the king said unto Araunah, Nay; but I will surely buy it of thee at a price: neither will I offer burnt-offerings unto the Lord my God of that which doth cost me nothing. So David bought the threshingfloor and the oxen for fifty shekels of silver. And David built there an altar unto the Lord, and offered burnt-offerings and peace-offerings. So the Lord was intreated for the land, and the plague was stayed from Israel."—II Samuel 24:18–25.

What a fine proposition that was which Araunah made to David! David might have the threshingfloor for building the altar, he might have oxen for the sacrifices, he might have the threshing implements for wood, so he could keep his obligation to God, offer the sacrifices, see the plague stopped in Israel, and all this without costing him a cent! An inexpensive way of serving God, wasn't it? But David would have none of it. He said, "Nay; but I will surely buy it of thee at a price: neither will I offer burnt-offerings unto the Lord my God of that which doth cost me nothing." David knew that to accept the land and the oxen and the wood free of charge, and then pretend that he was making an offering to God, would be insincere hypocrisy. David had many sins, but he did not have that one. He really meant business when he worshipped God.

So David bought the threshingfloor and the oxen for fifty shekels of silver, we are told. "And David built there an altar unto the Lord, and offered burnt-offerings and peace-offerings. So the Lord was intreated for the land, and the plague was stayed from Israel."

And you will be deeply interested, I am sure, when I tell you that God had had His eye on that very spot for hundreds of years. He had had Abraham take a three days' journey to offer Isaac there centuries ago. It was on that very spot that Solomon later built the temple. All this is clear in II Chronicles 3:1, which says, "Then Solomon began to build the house of the Lord at Jerusalem in mount Moriah, where the Lord appeared unto David his father, in the place that David had prepared in the threshingfloor of Ornan the Jebusite." Ornan was Araunah. And there in Mount Moriah, later called Mount Zion, the temple was built, and the Lord said, "For now have I chosen and sanctified this house, that my name may be there forever: and mine eyes and mine heart shall be there perpetually" (II Chron. 7:16).

David would never offer a burnt offering to the Lord of that which did not cost him anything. David was willing to pay the full price of discipleship.

From this text I want to bring a Bible message showing what it costs to be a good Christian, or the high cost of discipleship.

Please get it clear that I am not talking about what it costs to become a Christian. I am talking rather about what it costs to be a *good* Christian after you are already saved. There is a vast difference between just being a Christian, a converted man or woman saved by the blood, and being a really good Christian. For example, it is easy to get married. A girl can get married without money, without work; all she needs to do is say "Yes" and beat it to the office of the nearest Justice of the Peace or preacher! Multiplied thousands get married without ever having a serious thought about the matter, I fear. But after the girl is married, then to be a really good wife—that costs something! There is a vast difference between being converted, a child of God, and really serving God acceptably. So this message is not about how to be saved. It is about how to serve God after you are saved.

Let us have it settled to start with that salvation is free.

God's loving mercy and grace have provided salvation for all who will come to the Lord Jesus with a penitent heart and trust Him. You cannot buy salvation, you cannot earn it. You must accept it as God's free gift. It does not cost anything to be saved. All your labor, all your toil, all your sacrifice, all your tears, are utterly powerless and valueless to obtain salvation. The Bible plan of salvation is simply this, "For God so loved the world, that he gave his only begotten Son, that whosoever believeth in him should not perish, but have everlasting life" (John 3:16). It is stated again in the words of Paul and Silas to the jailor, "Believe on the Lord Jesus Christ, and thou shalt be saved" (Acts 16:31). After your sins are forgiven and your soul is saved, then, if you really want to serve God acceptably, you should expect to pay a price. Throughout the Bible is this solemn teaching, that those who serve the Lord should count the cost. All who would be good servants of Jesus Christ, acceptable preachers or missionaries or soul winners as lay Christians, all who would give a good testimony, must give and suffer and toil and be persecuted.

Are you trying to serve God today without its costing you anything? Do you offer to the Lord the kind of sacrifices that are really no sacrifices at all to you?

When Jesus told the disciples of His own impending trial and condemnation and crucifixion, He said, "If any man will come after me, let him deny himself, and take up his cross daily, and follow me. And whosoever will save his life shall lose it: but whosoever will lose his life for my sake, the same shall save it" (Luke 9:23, 24). If you expect a "Well done, thou good and faithful servant," when you meet the Saviour, you must be prepared to suffer for Him. The kind of service that does not cost anything is not worth anything and will not receive a reward when you meet the Saviour!

It appears that when it comes to the matter of salvation, there are two sides. On one side is the Lord Jesus, perfect, good, holy and merciful. And this righteous and holy Saviour did all the suffering, all the dying, and paid all the price that needs to be paid for the sinner's salvation. On the other side of the fence is the sinner. He is wholly wicked, there is nothing good about him to deserve salvation. All his righteousness is as filthy rags in God's sight (Isa. 64:6). His heart is deceitful above all things and desperately wicked, however nice he may appear to be outwardly (Jer. 17:9). All the sinner can do is to accept freely the wonderful salvation that is offered to him. Jesus does all the paying. Jesus does all the atoning. All the real work of salvation is done by the Lord Jesus Christ, and a sinner may accept it or reject it, but he cannot earn it.

But when the sinner trusts Christ for salvation and his sins are forgiven, all being charged against Jesus and paid for, then the Lord Jesus seems to tenderly invite him, saying, "Will you come now over to my side and help me bear the burden of the lost world? Will you come with Me, suffer with Me, follow Me, and help Me to get others saved?" So one who comes for his own salvation finds nothing he can do to earn it or to buy it or to deserve it. But after one is already saved, after one already receives the free salvation and is in Christ, then he may help the Lord Jesus bear the burden of a dying world.

Paul had this in mind when he said concerning himself, in Colossians 1:24, "Who now rejoice in my sufferings for you, and fill up that which is behind of the afflictions of Christ in my flesh for his body's sake, which is the church." Now that we are Christians we should live like Jesus lived. We should have the same mind that was in Christ Jesus; we should toil and be burdened for sinners and enter into all the reproach and labors of the Lord Jesus. It really costs something to be a good Christian! Salvation does not cost, but discipleship, that is, to be a real follower of Jesus, does cost greatly. Has it cost you to serve Christ?

I. What It Cost Bible Christians to Serve God

The marvelous unity of the Scriptures is nowhere better illustrated than in this fact, that in the Old Testament and New Testament alike—books written by some forty men under the Holy Spirit's direction, covering a period of fifteen centuries or more—we have a unanimous testimony that it costs much to be a real man or woman of God. It does not cost to be a Christian. It does greatly cost to be a *good* Christian.

1. Noah

Before the flood, Noah lived in a world given over to idolatry and license and violence, when every thought of the imagination of the hearts of men was evil and only evil continually. Noah preached one hundred and twenty years, preached in the power of the Holy Spirit, with no converts save his own wife, his three sons and their wives! Noah must have been known as the biggest nut the world had ever seen! He built an ocean liner of a boat, far from the sea, on high ground. He talked about a flood that would cover the highest mountains. And everybody knew that that was unscientific and impossible!

After the flood began nobody thought Noah was a fanatical fool! After the flood he was no longer in the minority but was in the majority! But do not think it was easy to build the ark and preach the gospel for a hundred and twenty years before the flood.

2. Abraham

Abraham's flocks and herds were enormous. He had 318 slaves who were trained soldiers (Gen. 14:14), perhaps a thousand other servants. Abraham would be a millionaire in any man's country. But obeying God, he left his father's country and his father's house. He went into a strange country where he was a sojourner, and there this man, who could have had a king's palace, lived the rest of his days in tents, with Sarah, called "Princess" and with Isaac, the son of his old age. Abraham, for the sake of his God, was willing to wait, for "he looked for a city which hath foundations, whose builder and maker is God" (Heb. 11:10). It cost Abraham all his kinspeople, most of the luxuries and some of the comforts of life, and caused him to wander in a strange land, that will one day, when Christ returns, belong to him.

3. *Jephthah*

Jephthah sacrificed his daughter according to his solemn vow made to the Lord. He promised God that if God would give him victory over the enemies of Israel, then the first thing that came to meet him out of his own house he would offer as a burnt offering. That first to greet him was his own daughter! Men greatly differ about whether Jephthah should have made such an awful vow, but whatever we think, this much is certain: Jephthah was not willing to serve God without it costing him something. He kept his vow to God, though with a broken heart. Jephthah meant business! Serving God aright, the death of his own daughter—that, Jephthah thought, was not too much for the God who heard his prayer and the God whom he served. Many of us have kept our children from God's service by our selfishness!

4. *Jeremiah*

Jeremiah served the Lord too. He was publicly slapped, he was jeered at and scorned. In prison he nearly starved to death in a muddy dungeon. Jeremiah, because he foretold the judgment of God on Jerusalem, because he kept warning the people that unless they should repent of their sins, ruin faced them, was hated and punished. It cost Jeremiah something to be true to God!

5. *Daniel and His Companions*

To serve God meant that Daniel should refuse to eat of the king's meat and the wine which was served him. He had to be an oddity, a back number, an 'old fogey.' Even when Daniel became famous and important, it cost him much to serve God. The conniving of his wicked enemies brought Daniel to where he must either quit his regular, thrice-daily prayer before the open windows towards Jerusalem, in effect deny his God, or he must go to the lions' den. So to the lions' den Daniel went. Let no one think it was easy. Daniel did not know whether he would return alive or not. Added to the persecution of his enemies, Daniel bore always the burden of a broken heart over Israel. He often fasted and prayed. He wept much before God. It is not an easy matter to be the kind of Christian that Daniel was.

The same thing is true of Shadrach, Meshach and Abed-nego, Daniel's companions. They were "religious fanatics," as was Daniel. They would not eat what other people ate, nor drink the wine that was furnished to the other young college men, their associates. When they were brought to the plain of Dura with the great multitude and were commanded to bow down before the great image set up by Nebuchadnezzar, they refused. When the instruments of music made their great sound, three Jewish boys stood bold upright, when everybody else bowed down to the image to please the king. The hot anger of the king threatened them with certain death in the fiery furnace if they did not bow before the idol, and they were given a second chance. Their stirring answer is in Daniel 3:16–18:

"O Nebuchadnezzar, we are not careful to answer thee in this matter. If it be so, our God whom we serve is able to deliver us from the burning fiery furnace, and he will deliver us out of thine hand, O king. But if not, be it known unto thee, O king, that we will not serve thy gods, nor worship the golden image which thou hast set up."

Oh the fury of Nebuchadnezzar, this first world ruler, when defied by three Jewish boys! The furnace was heated seven times hotter; they were bound and cast in. They trusted and hoped for deliverance, but they were ready to die. They were determined not to worship the idol god, whether God would deliver them or not. The fire did not harm them, but only burned their bonds, and the Lord Jesus Himself came and walked that day in the fiery furnace with these three who had served Him so faithfully! Who knows but that this sight of these faithful lads, coupled with Daniel's faithfulness, led King Nebuchadnezzar to the true God that day!

It was not easy to defy Nebuchadnezzar, to go against all the customs of the age and stand true to God, facing death for Him.

Do you think it ought to cost people less today to serve God?

6. Stephen

Stephen, like other Bible Christians, scorned to serve God in a way that would cost him nothing. Knowing where it would lead, Stephen preached the mighty sermon of Acts, chapter 7, when he was on trial for his life. Throwing aside his fears, he held up Jesus and condemned these men who had crucified Him.

"Then they cried out with a loud voice; and stopped their ears, and ran upon him with one accord, And cast him out of the city, and stoned him: and the witnesses laid down their clothes at a young man's feet, whose name was Saul. And they stoned Stephen, calling upon God, and saying, Lord Jesus, receive my spirit. And he kneeled down, and cried with a loud voice, Lord, lay not this sin to their charge. And when he had said this, he fell asleep."—Acts 7:57–60.

Oh, when I see Stephen in Heaven I hope I will not be ashamed! I hope that my kind of Christianity and his are the same kind, my devotion to Christ and his, alike. It cost Stephen being pounded to death with rocks, stoned to a bloody pulp in the dirt. Should it cost us nothing, then, to serve God?

7. Paul

Paul the apostle was an outstanding example of one who suffered for Christ. He had a tender, loving heart, but he never married. He gave up all thought of a home or a family for himself in order that he might give himself without any reserve to keeping souls out of Hell! What did it cost him? He tells us in II Corinthians 4:8–10,

"We are troubled on every side, yet not distressed; we are perplexed, but not in despair; Persecuted, but not forsaken; cast down, but not destroyed; Always bearing about in the body the dying of the Lord Jesus, that the life also of Jesus might be made manifest in our body."

Again he recounts, in II Corinthians 11:23–28, what it cost him to serve Christ.

"Are they ministers of Christ? (I speak as a fool) I am more; in labours more abundant, in stripes above measure, in prisons more frequent, in deaths oft. Of the Jews five times received I forty stripes save one. Thrice was I beaten with rods, once was I stoned, thrice I suffered shipwreck, a night and a day I have been in the deep; In journeyings often, in perils of waters, in perils of robbers, in perils by mine own countrymen, in perils by the heathen, in perils in the city, in perils in the wilderness, in perils in the sea, in perils among false brethren; In weariness and painfulness, in watchings often, in hunger and thirst, in fastings often, in cold and nakedness. Beside those things that are without, that which cometh upon me daily, the care of all the churches."

Paul was compelled to fight the wild beasts at Ephesus, probably in gladiatorial combat (I Cor. 15:32). From Damascus he fled for his life, being let down through a window in a basket outside the city wall (II Cor. 11:32, 33). At Lystra he was stoned and left for dead (Acts 14:19). Paul could say, "I bear in my body the marks of the Lord Jesus" (Gal. 6:17). All who would be Christians like Paul must expect that their service for God will cost them something. Oh for others who will live and labor and suffer like Paul, in order to win souls and serve the Lord in this wicked world!

All these were saved by simple faith in Christ. But they then proved good Christians, and it cost them much. I love to think of what a good time I will have in Heaven talking to Paul and Stephen, martyrs and heroes of the cross. I want Paul to tell me about the long years as a prisoner, with the chains on his hands and feet day and night. I would like for Paul to tell me about the day they led him out of Rome and chopped off his head. I shall ask Stephen to let me see some scars (if there could be any scars in Heaven) from the stones that had battered his face, broken his bones, and crushed his skull when he died outside Jerusalem, with his face like the face of an angel and with his voice pleading with God not to lay this sin to the charge of his murderers! But oh, what will I say if Stephen asks me to show him my scars! How can I hold up my end of the conversation if it centers around a life of sacrifice and toil and the loss of friendships and all things dear! What will I have to say about imprisonment, or poverty, or shame, or persecution; of actual hunger and beatings and chains, borne for Christ's sake?

How will I feel at home in Heaven with those saints described in the eleventh chapter of Hebrews, who lived in sheepskins and goatskins, who lived in caves and wandered in the mountains, who were sawn asunder, were burned at the stake, "of whom the world was not worthy"? How will I compare with those saints and martyrs? Oh, beloved Christians, if you want to shine in Heaven, then expect to pay a price for serving God in this world.

II. The Example of the Lord Jesus Teaches Us Sacrifice and Suffering

It is wonderful to call Christ Saviour. All those who put their trust in Him have a right to call Jesus Saviour and to call God "Our Father which art in Heaven." The smallest child, the newest convert, who has definitely accepted the pardon purchased for us on Calvary, can rightly call Jesus Saviour. But to call Him Lord is a different matter, and the Lord Jesus deserves to be Lord of all. If you call Jesus

Saviour, do you also call Him Lord? Is He your boss? Is He your example? Do you follow Him?

The example of the Lord Jesus teaches us that it should cost us something to serve God. How many Scriptures tell us to follow Christ, to be like Christ, to work like Christ! First Peter 2:21 says, "For even hereunto were ye called: because Christ also suffered for us, leaving us an example, that ye should follow his steps." Jesus suffered for us, and He left us an example that we should follow His steps! The novel by Charles M. Sheldon called *In His Steps, or What Would Jesus Do,* was based on this idea alone. Some 30 million copies have been printed, and millions have learned from it that every Christian should always try to do simply what he believes that Jesus Christ would do in his place. So Jesus suffered, and we should follow His example and suffer for Him, follow in His steps.

In Philippians 2:5–8 we are commanded to have the same attitude of mind that Jesus had.

"Let this mind be in you, which was also in Christ Jesus: Who, being in the form of God, thought it not robbery to be equal with God: But made himself of no reputation, and took upon him the form of a servant, and was made in the likeness of men: And being found in fashion as a man, he humbled himself, and became obedient unto death, even the death of the cross."

We are to have the mind of Christ. And this mind of Christ led Him to give up Heaven for the earth; led Him to give up His will for the Father's will; made Him obedient to death, even the death of the cross! That suggests that a life of burden, of self-surrender and suffering awaits those who truly have the mind of Christ, who follow in His steps. In John 14:12 we are told, "He that believeth on me, the works that I do shall he do also." In John 20:21 we read that Jesus told the disciples, "As my Father hath sent me, even so send

I you." In John 15:18 we are told, "If the world hate you, ye know that it hated me before it hated you." And in John 15:20 the Saviour continued on the same theme, saying, "Remember the word that I said unto you, The servant is not greater than his lord. If they have persecuted me, they will also persecute you; if they have kept my saying, they will keep your's also."

Oh, dear Christian, do you believe that you are any better than your Master, the Lord Jesus? If He suffered, should you not suffer, too? If people hated Him, then would they not hate you, too, if you were like Him and if you were near Him?

Thomas Shepherd wrote:

> Must Jesus bear the cross alone,
> And all the world go free?
> No; there's a cross for every one,
> And there's a cross for me.

And remember that Isaac Watts wrote,

> Must I be carried to the skies,
> On flowery beds of ease,
> While others fought to win the
> prize,
> And sailed through bloody seas?
>
> Sure I must fight if I would reign:
> Increase my courage, Lord!
> I'll bear the toil, endure the pain,
> Supported by Thy word.

The example of the Lord Jesus proves that any Christian who really serves God must expect to pay a heavy cost. It does not cost to get saved, but oh, it does cost to serve the Lord Jesus acceptably and do the work that He has left us to do.

III. What It Ought to Cost A Christian to Serve God

Let us prayerfully consider just what it ought to cost to be a good Christian. What ought it to cost one to serve God with all of his heart?

1. It Ought to Cost Money to Serve God

When David said, "Nay; but I will surely buy it of thee at a price: neither will I offer burnt-offerings unto the Lord my God of that which doth cost me nothing," he referred to actual cash money. And he bought the threshingfloor and the oxen for fifty shekels of silver. That suggests that Christians ought always to expect it to cost money to serve God.

Now I believe that preachers ought not to set any particular price on their services, and I believe they ought to be willing to trust God completely about these matters. Many preachers have greatly hindered their ministry by being too much concerned about what they should receive. But at the same time it would be a grievous sin for a preacher not to teach the people what God says about giving. People ought to be taught that serving God acceptably includes a cost in dollars and cents.

Some preachers, in order to be independent and not be accused of commercialism, have made their own living and have preached on the side without salary. But in every such case, as far as I know, the churches failed to prosper. Christians were not taught to serve God with a whole heart.

Many pastors say that they are embarrassed to take offerings or collections in church services, and many a pastor has said, "I wish it were never necessary." But that attitude is wrong. I believe that people ought to be taught that giving is right. The work does not need the money so much as people need to give. To give money for the service of Christ and to get out the gospel is a great privilege and a pastor would sin against his people if he did not give them that opportunity and teach them of this blessing and this grace. How I thank God for the day I learned that I could safely trust Him with the tithes and offerings and that He would look after my needs! Oh, how much people lose by not putting God first on the money question!

But in these fat days of war salaries when anybody can get

a well paid job, no matter how poor his training nor how ordinary his work, I fear that most of us do not know anything about real sacrifice. The churches, it may be, have plenty of money for their needs, and preachers get salaries enough, perhaps; but I fear that the money that is given is largely just a surplus and does not represent any sacrifice. What we give to God is too often just incidental, merely "chicken feed" like the tips we give a redcap or porter or waitress; like the money so carelessly spent for an evening's entertainment, or for a soda, or newspaper, or shoe shine, or carfare. To the average Christian, I fear his giving is only an incidental matter. The average Christian has just as much to eat as he would have if he did not give his dime or dollar or several dollars to the church. The average Christian wears just as nice clothes as if he did not give God a cent. All the money the average Christian gives to take the gospel to the whole world, for the support of all the orphans and Christian poor, for missions at home and abroad, and for his local church, does not mean that he ever has to do without dessert or postpone the buying of a suit, or do without a new car!

I remember the days of my poverty-stricken boyhood near a little west Texas cow town. The pastor in the little Baptist church preached two Sundays a month and the other two Sundays he preached in another town. Comparing what I remember of his sermons with those I hear today, I am convinced that he was a profound Bible preacher who preached with a pathos and fervor, as well as with solid doctrine, that might well be the envy of pastors in many great pulpits today. Naturally his pay was small. I recall that for four years he wore the same blue serge suit, winter and summer. On week days at home he wore overalls, but that blue serge suit was his winter suit and his summer suit. It was worn slick.

Once a great rally of Baptist people was planned for our part of the state, at Wichita Falls. A group of church members, with loving devotion, talked among themselves and raised twenty dollars to give dear Brother Longan for a new suit. How proud he was of that suit he planned to get! In Archer City, where he lived, nothing could be found to suit his taste. If you only buy one suit in four years, and have only twenty dollars for it, you can be particular. So the dear man of God waited until he went to Wichita Falls. He thought, "Between services I will go to the stores and find just the suit I want for my twenty dollars." But in the services missionaries were on the program. One missionary told of the lost, unreached millions of China. He said that approximately one-fourth of the population of the whole earth was there and that the vast majority of them had never even heard about Jesus Christ! He told of the hunger of heart he had found, and oh, how badly new missionaries were needed! He said that young men and women were ready if only the money could be found to send them. A collection was taken and this dear preacher said, "Lord, this suit I have has lasted me for four years and it can do another year. I am not going to have a new suit if it may mean that somebody in China will never hear the gospel and will go to Hell." So he put the whole twenty dollars in the offering. How proudly and gladly he wore that same shiny blue serge back to his home and then to his churches to preach the gospel!

And I tell you, Christians, we who must have dessert on the table every day, must have hardwood floors and tile baths, and deep piled rugs, and pleasant window drapes and nice cars, and fine clothes and meat at every meal--I tell you that one day the uncounted millions of the lost who have never heard the gospel will rise up against us in the judgment to accuse us that our giving never really meant anything! They will say that it never cost us anything to serve God! Our comforts and luxuries we value more than keeping souls out of an eternal Hell!

If you have as much to eat and wear as you would have without giving, then certainly you have not given enough. Oh that we might love the Lord Jesus enough that it would really cost us something in money!

2. Serving God Ought to Cost a Christian Much Time and Labor

Paul said he was "in labours more abundant." He told the elders at Ephesus that "by the space of three years I ceased not to warn every one night and day with tears" (Acts 20:31). He often labored with his own hands, not only making a living for himself but providing for the needs of his workers.

Moses carried the heavy burden of the responsibility for the whole nation of Israel. He likened it to carrying them all, as a nursing father would, in his arms.

Whoever understood the real labor and toil of the Saviour! He was driven night and day by His loving urge to do the will of the Father, to fulfill the Scriptures, to help the sick and sinning, to save souls. "My Father worketh hitherto, and I work" (John 5:17). Jesus had a crisis to meet, a crucifixion to suffer, an atonement to accomplish, and He said, "How am I straitened till it be accomplished!" (Luke 12:50).

So does it seem strange if God demands a man's time and labor? Our church rolls today are filled largely with people who only attend services occasionally without any of the sweat and labor of getting people saved. How many do house-to-house visiting, earnestly seeking to win souls day after day? How many give much time to study and prayer and waiting on God and really teaching the Word of God to everyone who will hear?

Once I was assistant pastor of a fine church, and in my hands were placed some of the financial arrangements of the church. A well-to-do Christian man in the church instructed me to simply write a check on his account each week for a certain amount for the church budget. For some weeks I followed that plan, then I quit it. I thought that any man who wanted to give money to the Lord's cause ought to give more attention and time to the matter than that. After the first of the month he reproached me, saying, "Brother Rice, I find that no checks have been drawn on my account this month for the

Lord's work. Go ahead and write a check for me each week. I am glad to give the money. I just simply do not like to take the time to think of it each week and give attention to the matter. I am glad for you to write the checks and I am glad to give the money."

I replied, "If you cannot give God enough time to even write your own checks for His cause, I do not think He wants your money. You can write your own checks, or the church will do without your offerings." Why should God want anybody's money when He doesn't have enough of one's interest and time to even write a check or to turn the money over to the Lord's cause?

Remember that the Saviour said in Luke 10:2, "The harvest truly is great, but the labourers are few: pray ye therefore the Lord of the harvest, that he would send forth labourers into his harvest." God demands your toil and your time. Your best thought, your most earnest labor, the longest hours are all too little to give to the Lord Jesus who bought you and paid for you with His own blood.

3. Serving God Ought to Cost a Christian the Affection of Friends and Loved Ones

Some people have the foolish idea that to be a really good Christian makes everybody love you, but that is false. The better Christian you are, the more people will treat you as they treated the Lord Jesus. Men hated Him, lied about Him, tried to throw Him over a cliff, tried to stone Him. Later, when God's time was come, they were allowed to spit in His face, to pluck out His beard, to hit Him over the head with a reed when He was blindfolded, saying, "Prophesy . . . who . . . smote thee." He was beaten with a Roman scourge, stripped of His garments, and nailed to a Roman cross where the howling crowd mocked Him while He died. Remember that Jesus said, "If the world hate you, ye know that it hated me before it hated you." The right kind of a Christian will lose friends for Jesus.

I was greatly impressed when I heard Dr. Louis T. Talbot,

President of Los Angeles Bible Institute, say, "I thank God for my friends, and I thank God for my enemies!"

Joseph's brethren hated him and sold him into slavery. Daniel's fellow governors hated him and planned to have him slain. They had him cast into the lions' den but God delivered him. The priests of Baal hated Elijah, and Jezebel swore to kill him because he denounced her idolatry. Herodias hated John the Baptist because he condemned her adultery, and Herod cut off his head. The Pharisees and the Judaizers hated Paul with a burning hatred, and forty men took an oath they would neither eat nor drink until they slew him! This idea that the better Christian you are, the milder and gentler you will be and the more everybody will love you, is a false idea, contrary to the Scriptures.

Now and then people say about some preacher, "He hasn't an enemy in the world." If that be true about any preacher, then God pity him; he has not been true to Christ, for Jesus said:

> *"Blessed are they which are persecuted for righteousness' sake: for their's is the kingdom of heaven. Blessed are ye, when men shall revile you, and persecute you, and shall say all manner of evil against you falsely, for my sake. Rejoice, and be exceeding glad: for great is your reward in heaven: for so persecuted they the prophets which were before you."* —Matt. 5:10–12.

Along with the pure in heart, the meek, they that hunger and thirst after righteousness, the peacemakers, Jesus blessed those who are talked about, those who lose their friends, those who are hated and persecuted for His sake!

I say, any man who lives for Christ like he ought to will lose friends. If you do not believe it, then you should hear how those who claim sinless perfection talk about Dr. Ironside who found himself "only holy in spots," as he said, and ceased to claim "entire sanctification," and "the eradication of the carnal nature" as they did.

You should hear what tavern keepers, brewers and distillers, with some drunkards and their political friends, say about Dr. Sam Morris, *The Voice of Temperance* broadcaster!

You should hear what Seventh Day Adventists and so-called Christian Scientists say about Dr. Louis T. Talbot, who has so well exposed their un-Christian doctrines.

You should hear what modernist leaders in the American Baptist Convention say about Dr. Robert Ketcham, who has led in the organization of the Association of Regular Baptist Churches, a group of Baptists who are fundamental in doctrine. Or you should hear what these same modernistic Baptists say about Dr. W. B. Riley, that staunch heroic statesman who stayed within the convention until shortly before he died, but fought the infidelity in it and got Baptists of Minnesota to withdraw support from a modernistic college, and from the National Council of Churches!

You should hear what the modernist bishops and infidel preachers in modern Methodism say about Dr. Bob Shuler of Trinity Methodist Church, Los Angeles, because he constantly tries to bring Methodists back to the old-time Bible religion of salvation by the blood.

D. L. Moody was called "crazy Moody" by Chicago preachers.

Charles H. Spurgeon, the greatest Baptist preacher who ever lived, was largely ostracized by the Baptists of Great Britain, and he withdrew from the denomination because of what he called "the down-grade movement," away from the inspiration of the Bible.

John Wesley, an Episcopal clergyman, educated in Oxford, was shut out of his own church and preached instead to the assembled multitudes who gathered around as he stood upon his father's tombstone!

Billy Sunday, who was used of God to win hundreds of thousands of souls, was criticised by the mass of preachers over America as a mountebank, as a moneygrabber, as a sensationalist.

Dr. R. A. Torrey, one of the greatest evangelists and greatest Bible teachers America has ever known, the man who set up the curriculum and was the first dean at Moody Bible Institute, the man who later did the same thing for Los Angeles Bible Institute and founded the Church of the Open Door, is even today, though in glory, called a fanatic on the Holy Spirit by multitudes of so-called Bible teachers who never had a great revival and who rarely, if ever, win a soul!

Men who preach as Elijah did against idolatry, as John the Baptist did against adultery, as Paul did against religious formalism and salvation by works, or as Stephen did about those who reject Christ, will lose friends. Jesus said, "I came not to send peace, but a sword" (Matt. 10:34). He said, "A man's foes shall be they of his own household" (Matt. 10:36). He said to His disciples, "Ye shall be hated of all nations for my name's sake" (Matt. 24:9). Do you think, then, that a Christian who lives as close to God as he ought, and who really does the will of God, will never lose any friends?

Some girl who reads this, if she really laid her life all on the altar for God, would break an unholy engagement with someone who is not a Christian, and whom, therefore, she has no right to marry. A few weeks ago a young woman sadly told me that she was not coming back to college. She was engaged to be married to an unconverted soldier; she loved him and would not give him up. So she found no pleasure in trying to serve God and she felt that study in a Christian college was useless since she had determined to go contrary to God's will in that matter. How much better if she had taken her loss, endured her broken heart, and had the Lord comfort her and adjust her life to His own sweet plan! As it is now, if she follows her present plan, she will have a lifetime of trouble, and meet the Lord Jesus ashamed because she was not true to Him, though she was saved and truly loves Him.

Someone who reads this would, no doubt, be fired from your position if you stood up for Jesus and lived out-and-out for Him down where you work, as you ought to do. Some of you would be thought "a religious fanatic" and people would say that you were "gone crazy about the Bible," or that you were "a holy roller" if you really set out to talk about the Lord Jesus as much as you ought, and if you tried as hard as He wants you to do, to win souls to Him.

Dear reader, what kind of a Christian are you? Did you ever lose a job, or lose a night's sleep, or lose a friend for God? If your Christianity never cost you a dollar, never cost you a friend, never cost any tears or broken heart, then can you really say that you love the Lord very much? To be a really good Christian is going to cost you friends.

We are told that the Saviour left Heaven and "made himself of no reputation" (Phil. 2:7). Do you think, then, that we ought to keep all of our reputation? Don't you think that some of us ought to be willing to lose out with friends and bear the reproach of Christ? If you please everybody else, you cannot please the Lord Jesus. For remember it is written, "Ye adulterers and adulteresses, know ye not that the friendship of the world is enmity with God? whosoever therefore will be a friend of the world is the enemy of God" (James 4:4).

4. Serving God Should Cost a Christian the Giving Up of His Whole Life's Plan, the Surrender to Christ of All Control

How much does God require of a Christian? Some say that God requires one-tenth of his income. Some say that God requires one-seventh of his time. Actually, that does not express what God requires at all. The tithe and the offerings which God says belong to Him are only a token payment. Rather, we should realize that not one-tenth but ten-tenths of all we have belong to God. Not one day out of seven, but all of the seven days belong to God. As stated in Romans 12:1, God's requirement is this, "I beseech you therefore, brethren, by the mercies of God, that ye present your bodies a living sacrifice, holy, acceptable unto God, which is your reasonable service." God requires no less than the complete surrender of all control over your own life. It is only when you have taken up your cross to follow Jesus to Calvary and there counted self dead, that you are fit to come and "follow me," as Jesus said in Luke 9:23. And remember that He said this is to be done every day!

That is the reason Paul said, "I die daily" (I Cor. 15:31). Paul simply meant that he had given himself up to die. He was willing to die any day that came along, and prepared to die. In fact, eventually he did have his head cut off. That was no shock, no surprise to Paul. He had been surrendered to that, had been planning for that since the day on the road to Damascus when he gave himself up to Jesus and said, "Lord, what wilt thou have me to do?"

God may want to change your plans completely as He changed mine when He called me from being a college teacher to be a preacher of the gospel. God may call you from the comforts of America to live and teach and toil and win and then die in some mud-hut in black Africa! God may call you from being loved and respected, to be an outcast among your own friends and thought a fool by your family. He may call you from wealth down to a life of poverty. To be sure, there will be the sweetness of His presence all the way. To be sure, there will be a marvelous reward in Heaven. To be sure, the ways of the Lord Jesus are ways of pleasantness and His paths are paths of peace. His way is always best. It always pays to follow the sweet leading of His Spirit, the holy compulsion of His word. But I tell you frankly that He has the right and demands that you recognize it—the right to tell you where to live, what to do, whom to marry or not to marry, how to live, when to die. No one can really serve the Lord Jesus adequately, completely, until he can lay everything on the altar and say, "Not my will, but Thine be done," as the Saviour Himself said. Actually God demands the complete surrender. He wants all that you have and all you are.

C. T. Studd in England had inherited wealth. He had fame as the greatest athlete of his day. He had social standing. Practically anything in England that he wanted he could have. Yet he gave up his cricket playing, went to China as a missionary, gave away all his fortune deliberately and carefully, and then gave himself to a life of self-renunciation and self-denial to get the gospel to poor sinners. He served in China, later he went into the interior of Africa and opened a new mission field. For some fourteen years he was kept away from wife and child by the call of preaching the gospel to the heathen. At last he died, away in the interior of Africa. Career and fortune had early gone on the altar. Health and home and family life went also. Indeed C. T. Studd once said, "I have searched into my life and I do not know of anything else left that I can sacrifice to the Lord Jesus Christ."

I say to you, God requires the same surrender of you as He required of C. T. Studd. It may not be Africa for you, but it means exactly the same surrender. I do not know whether you ought to give away all your money, but I know that you ought to be willing to do it any minute that you find it would please the Lord Jesus.

It is my prayer that hundreds who read this message may this very day and hour make a holy renunciation of your own plans and say a glad eternal "yes" to all that God will ask of you.

Mary Brown wrote,

> It may not be on the mountain height,
>   Or over the stormy sea;
> It may not be at the battle's front
>   My Lord will have need of me;
> But if, by a still, small voice He calls
>   To paths that I do not know,
> I'll answer, dear Lord, with my hand in Thine,
>   I'll go where you want me to go.
>
> Perhaps today there are loving words
>   Which Jesus would have me speak;
> There may be now in the paths of sin,
>   Some wand'rer whom I should seek:

O Saviour, if Thou wilt be my Guide,
  Though dark and rugged the way,
My voice shall echo the message sweet,
  I'll say what you want me to say.

There's surely somewhere a lowly place
  In earth's harvest fields so wide,
Where I may labor through life's short day
  For Jesus, the Crucified;
So trusting my all to Thy tender care,
  And knowing Thou lovest me,
I'll do Thy will with a heart sincere,
  I'll be what you want me to be.

I'll go where you want me to go, dear Lord,
  Over mountain, or plain, or sea;
I'll say what you want me to say, dear Lord,
  I'll be what you want me to be.

IV. Whatever It Costs to Serve God Must Be Voluntary

David said, "Nay; but I will surely buy it of thee at a price: neither will I offer burnt-offerings unto the Lord my God of that which doth cost me nothing." David was not under necessity of buying the threshingfloor. Araunah was willing to give it freely. He did not need to buy the fat oxen for the sacrifice. Araunah offered them as one king to another! But David refused to have these without a price. David would not offer to the Lord his God a burnt-offering that did not cost him something. David that day expressed the principle that all acceptable service to God comes from a willing, glad heart. Nobody can serve God acceptably except as that service is voluntary.

Moses gave up the place as the son of Pharaoh's daughter; perhaps he gave up a chance to be king of Egypt. But remember that Moses made his own choice, "Choosing rather to suffer affliction with the people of God, than to enjoy the pleasures of sin for a season" (Heb. 11:25).

Do you think that Daniel could not have avoided the lions' den if he had not been willing to go there? He did not need to go before his open window to pray. And the three Hebrew companions of Daniel had a second chance to bow down to the great image set up by Nebuchadnezzar had they wanted to save their lives that way.

Stephen was not compelled to stand and preach to the Pharisees when he was arrested, so accusing them straightly of the crucifixion of Christ that they killed him. Paul knew ahead of time that "bonds and afflictions" awaited him at Jerusalem, yet he went on steadfastly there (Acts 20:23).

Sometimes people say that in olden times God wanted some people to die for Him, but that now He does not want anybody to die as a martyr; He simply wants people to live for Him. But I find no teaching like that in the Bible. God has not changed His plans. Somebody ought to die for the Lord Jesus these days, and if we loved Him enough and if we were as true to Him as we ought to be, some of us, doubtless, would. But do you suppose that anybody was ever burned at the stake who was just a casual, ordinary Christian, like most of us are? Certainly not! Christians who never win a soul, who never fight some great iniquity, who never oppose false doctrines, who never risk all in an attack on the forces of evil —such Christians of course will never die for Jesus. If you do not give Satan any trouble, then of course Satan will not worry much about you. They never piled any fagots nor set any fires burning around ordinary Christians who lived like the rest of the world and simply went to church occasionally! The only people who were ever worthy to be martyred were those who set out to die, if need be, in order to carry out the plan of Christ and to save souls.

A friend of mine who was an orthodox Jew, born in Russia, came to America to get away from the pogroms in Russia, where his father, a Jewish rabbi, was slain. He himself had spent eight years in study of the Talmud, planning to be a rabbi. So he taught in the Chicago Hebrew Institute. The Holy Spirit sought this Jew, led him from Chicago to Dallas and from Dallas to Fort Worth, where eventually he could not get away from the Hebrew Scriptures that foretold the coming of the Saviour. I saw him stand one day in the Southwestern Baptist Theological Seminary chapel to tell how at two o'clock that morning he had surrendered his heart and life and all to the Lord Jesus Christ.

With child-like simplicity this Jew set out to serve the Lord. He came to my home often. I remember the day when he brought me a letter. His face was gray, his hand trembled; it was from his baby sister whom he had brought from Russian Poland and had supported in America. He translated the letter from Yiddish for me, and this is about what it said:

"Dear Louis:—

"Sister and I are greatly distressed at the insane thing that has happened to you. Who ever thought that you would become a traitor to your father and your father's religion, a renegade Jew! Oh, leave your bastard Christ and come back to us and be happy again!"

He had been a father to those younger sisters, but with trembling lips and hoarse voice he said, "Brother Rice, I cannot give up my Saviour! I love my sisters—I have supported them ever since my father died. I have given them all my money and tried to make them happy. This breaks my heart; but I cannot give up my Saviour!"

Later he brought me another letter from the same sister. He had written his two sisters urging them to accept the Saviour. The reply was something like this:

"You are no longer a brother of mine. Already we have counted you dead. The rabbi has conducted funeral services for you. We have gone through the apartment and sought out everything that had your name on it and every gift you ever bought for us, and have destroyed them. The only thing that remains is this fountain pen you gave me on my last birthday. When I have finished this letter and signed my name, I will stamp the pen to pieces on the floor and throw the pieces in the garbage. You traitor Jew, you may have your bastard Christ! You are no brother of ours any more!"

That was hard for my Jewish friend to bear. Remember

that a Jew is not received very warmly even by Christians. They never forget that he is a Jew, they never forgive him his idiosyncrasies and peculiarities. The average Christian is not very kind to a Jewish Christian; yet my friend steadfastly refused to go back to his family. His surrender to Jesus was voluntary. He had counted the cost and he, having put his hand to the plow, did not look back! I believe that that is the kind of service God wants.

A few years ago a young couple went to China as missionaries. First Betty Scott went with her father, a Presbyterian missionary. She had been educated in an American college and at Moody Bible Institute. There she had fallen in love with John Stam. And John loved her with all his heart. They hoped and prayed and dreamed that God would allow them to live and work together. John was accepted as a missionary and went to China. There he saw Betty again, and soon they were married. In a year God sent a lovely baby, Priscilla. Then they went into the interior to open a new field. Soon communistic bandits came to take the town and sack it. They took John and Betty Stam and cut off their heads. Only the baby, Priscilla, lived to be brought back to America.

Many people thought, "Oh, what a tragedy!" No doubt many said, "What a waste of young lives and talent and training!" I can well imagine that some people thought, "Oh, if John and Betty had known the terrible cost, I wonder if they would have gone to China?"

Well, happily, I can answer that question. Do you suppose that God would take people to a martyr's death when they had not themselves surrendered to Him? Oh, no! Dr. Scott, Betty's father, sat by me at the faculty table for lunch at Moody Bible Institute several years ago and showed me a Bible that had been recovered many months after this martyrdom from Betty's effects, stolen by the communists. In the back of this Bible which he, Dr. Scott, had given to his daughter when she was a sophomore in college, he showed me in Betty's handwriting this solemn vow:

"MY COVENANT"

"Lord, I give up my own purposes and plans, all my own desires, hopes and ambitions (whether they be fleshly or soulish), and accept Thy will for my life. I give myself, my life, my all, utterly to Thee, to be Thine forever. I hand over to Thy keeping all of my friendships, my love.

"All the people whom I love are to take second place in my heart.

"Fill me and seal me with Thy Holy Spirit. Work out Thy whole will in my life, at any cost, now and forever. 'To me to live is Christ and to die is gain' (Phil. 1:21).

"Elizabeth Alden Scott
August 3, 1925."

So I was not surprised when I read excerpts from the diary of John Stam, her young husband, and found that he, too, had made a definite covenant, years before when he was a student at the Moody Bible Institute, asking God to glorify Himself in his young life "whether by life or by death." These two young people had a rendezvous with death. They had offered themselves for martyrdom. God in His infinite mercy granted to them that high and holy privilege, to die for the gospel. How high their honor! How great their reward! Remember it was voluntary. They gave themselves up to die for Jesus, and He accepted their gracious surrender and set His seal upon it and blessed it!

I do not know what God's will is for you. But I know that today you ought to lay your life, your family, your career, your time, your money, your talents,—all you are or can be —on the altar for Jesus Christ.

How many will say today like David "Nay; but I will surely buy it of thee at a price: neither will I offer burnt-offerings unto the Lord my God of that which doth cost me nothing"? I pray that many will decide and write today to tell me what you have decided to do that will really cost something for Christ. Let me counsel with those who are now surrendering for the ministry or the mission field. I will gladly advise about going to college or Bible institute or seminary.

2

Outside the Gate with Jesus

"We have an altar, whereof they have no right to eat which serve the tabernacle. For the bodies of those beasts, whose blood is brought into the sanctuary by the high priest for sin, are burned without the camp. Wherefore Jesus also, that he might sanctify the people with his own blood, suffered without the gate. Let us go forth therefore unto him without the camp, bearing his reproach. For here have we no continuing city, but we seek one to come."

—Hebrews 13:10–14.

WHEN the book of Hebrews was written about 64 A.D., the temple was still standing and all the ceremonial sacrifices were offered regularly, just as they had been before Christ came. A little later, in 70 A.D., Titus, the Roman general, would besiege the city and take it and destroy it, and the temple would not have one stone left upon another. Jews would be scattered all over the world and the Levitical offerings brought to an end. But when the Scripture text above was written the sin offerings referred to were still brought to the temple for sacrifices; the blood was sprinkled before the altar of incense in the sanctuary and then what was left was poured out at the big brazen altar. Then the body of the bullock was taken outside the gate and burned.

The reader will remember that the priests and the Levites had their food from the offerings brought to the temple. Parts or all of many sacrifices were given to the priests and Levites for food. But they had no right to eat of this bullock whose body must be taken outside the gate and burned. And the inspired author of the epistle to the Hebrews tells us that God meant by this to teach that Spirit-filled Christians have a blessed privilege which is here pictured, of going outside the gate of human approval with the rejected and crucified Saviour. That body of the bullock, burned outside the gate, pictured the crucified and rejected Saviour. It also pictures the Spirit-filled Christian.

The Christian does not belong to this world. To be sure a Christian should do his duty as husband, father, mother, child, citizen, pupil, in relation to other people. The Christian should be a good citizen of this world. But the Christian should remember, "Our citizenship is in Heaven." The Christian should sing

> I am a pilgrim, I am a stranger
> I can tarry, I can tarry but a night.

Or in the words of a popular gospel folk-song,

> This world is not my home,
> I'm just a passing through
> My treasures are laid up
> Somewhere beyond the blue.
> The angels beckon me
> From Heaven's open door
> And I can't feel at home
> In this world anymore.

The Christian should be different from the worldling.

The good Christian should be like an American ambassador in Moscow, Russia. He should mean well to Russia, should strive to be a help, and yet he would be out of place, would not be at home, would be misunderstood and probably unwelcome, and he might be abused or insulted or even killed. The Christian in this world is on enemy territory. He has blessings the rest of the world does not know about and has privileges which they will not accept.

There is a Bible doctrine of separation throughout even the Old Testament. A Jew was not to plow with the ox and the ass hitched together (Deut. 22:10). He was thus reminded that a Jew was different from a Gentile. A Jew could not eat what a Gentile ate. A Jew could not worship what a Gentile worshipped. A Jew was not to intermarry with Gentiles. And the ceremonial law reminded the Hebrew in a hundred ways of the fact that he was a separate kind of person. The Jewish boy was circumcised when he was eight days old as a brand and mark that he was different from the Gentile. He was not to wear a garment of linen and woolen together. He was not to plant a vineyard with diverse kinds of seed (Deut. 22:9, 11). God meant that to be a spiritual lesson to Christians. We are different, too. God grant we may not be ashamed to be different, and to show ourselves more pleasing to Heaven than to this present wicked world.

The text above, Hebrews 13:10, says that "we have an altar, whereof they have no right to eat which serve the tabernacle."

Jewish priests were in the city, honored and respected. Christians should go outside the gate of worldly esteem. The world likes very well a religion which puts Jews, Protestants, Catholics, and non-Christian Masons on the same plane. The world doesn't mind your believing there is a God. The world does mind a Christian insisting that the atoning blood of Jesus Christ is the only way to keep out of Hell! The world does mind the Christian saying that the only God is the God of the Bible, that there is no salvation except through Jesus Christ, that this salvation is to be received wholly by faith in Christ. The world does not mind one saying that everybody should follow the Sermon on the Mount. A whisky-drinking, poker-playing, profane president mentions that as a matter of course, without repentance, without breaking from his gangster-ridden political machine, without turning from his socialism demagoguery. But a red-hot evangelism, demanding that men everywhere repent and turn to Christ for salvation, is offensive to this world.

The Christian here is offered the privilege of being different from the nominal Christian. There was a difference between Abraham and Lot, though both were doubtless saved men. Abraham was spiritual, Lot was worldly. There was a difference between King Saul and King David, though God had given Saul also a new heart, we are told. There was a difference between Paul and Barnabas on the one hand, filled with the Spirit and going on a great missionary journey that might bring death and, on the other hand, John Mark, whose heart failed him so that he left the evangelistic party and went home to his mother! There was a difference between Paul the apostle, waiting to be offered as a sacrifice at Rome, and Demas who forsook Paul, "having loved this present world" (II Tim. 4:10).

Paul made it very clear that this spiritual difference existed between him and most of the Christians at Corinth. Paul wrote them:

"Now ye are full, now ye are rich, ye have reigned as kings without us: and I would to God ye did reign, that we also might reign with you. For I think that God hath set forth us the apostles last, as it were appointed to death: for we are made a spectacle unto the world, and to angels, and to men. We are fools for Christ's sake, but ye are wise in Christ; we are weak, but ye are strong; ye are honourable, but we are despised. Even unto this present hour we both hunger, and thirst, and are naked, and are buffeted, and have no certain dwellingplace; And labour, working with our own hands: being reviled, we bless; being persecuted, we suffer it: Being defamed, we entreat: we are made as the filth of the world, and are the offscouring of all things unto this day."—I Cor. 4:8–13.

The Christians at Corinth were full and rich while Paul was poor. They were wise in the sight of the world which counted Paul a fool. They were strong in the sight of the world to whom Paul appeared weak. They were honorable, but Paul was despised. Paul was defamed and made as the filth of the world and the offscouring of all things. It was because Paul learned to eat of the sacrifice mentioned in our text, willing to go outside the gate with Christ, bearing His reproach.

I remember how strange it seemed to me, when I was a pastor of a church, that many pastors and churches thought me an extremist, yet liked the kind of Christians my preaching and training produced. We were counted rather radical. One could not teach in our Sunday School without having a very high standard of godly living. One who attended the movies or danced or played bridge or used tobacco was not, we thought, a good enough Christian to be a teacher and example to young people. We taught that every Christian should be an earnest and loving student of the Word of God, that every Christian should be a soul winner. I preached boldly and plainly against modernism, against Christians being yoked up with unbelievers in secret orders. All this seemed very radical to many pastors and church leaders around us. Yet we discovered that they prized most highly every member they could get from our church. Sometimes a member would come to one of these churches from our church and would immediately be put to teaching an adult class, though they might not have been counted worthy to teach children in our church.

In that church where the blessing of God dwelt, many a drunkard was made sober, many a miserable home was made happy. The business world was glad to give jobs to the drunkards we had won to Christ and saw transformed. Families on relief got converted, were cleaned up, got good jobs, made respectable citizens, took places of leadership and grew into places of respect and honor in the community. The world liked our converts, though it did not like the preacher! They were honorable but we were despised. The world would like to have the transformed lives which radical, Spirit-filled Christianity can furnish. The world would like to have the fruits without the Spirit-filled, sin-condemning gospel which brings the fruits. People would like to have the blessings of Christ without the reproach of Christ.

But here God is calling us to go the second mile. God wants us not only to have life, but to have it more abundantly. He wants us not only to drink for ourselves but to be a fountain of living water to others. God wants us to have not only the richness and glory of Christ, but His poverty, His reproach.

I. The Sacrifice Picturing the Atoning Work of Christ

1. Every Bloody Sacrifice of the Old Testament Pictures Jesus Christ

When Abraham and his son Isaac crawled up the slope of Mount Moriah, carrying the wood and the fire, innocent Isaac asked with boyish curiosity, "Behold the fire and the wood: but where is the lamb for a burnt-offering?" Abraham with a double meaning responded, "My son, God will provide himself a lamb for a burnt-offering" (Gen. 22:7, 8). God provided a lamb for an offering that day, in the place of Isaac; they found a ram caught in a thicket by his horns and offered him. But Abraham knew that God would also one day offer His own Son, the Lamb of God. That is why Jesus said, "Abraham saw my day . . . and was glad" (John 8:56).

The New Testament tells us that the passover lamb, when offered at a certain time each year by every Jewish family, pictured Christ. "For even Christ our passover is sacrificed for us" (I Cor. 5:7). When John the Baptist saw Jesus as He walked, he said, "Behold the Lamb of God, which taketh away the sin of the world" (John 1:29). Every sacrifice was an object lesson that prophesied that God would send His Son to pay for man's sin.

Each sacrifice had a different lesson. How many, many illustrations it would take to properly picture the wonderful work of Jesus Christ! The bullock pictured Christ as the burden-bearing Saviour. The turtle dove pictured Him as the mourning One, despised and rejected of men. The pure white pigeon pictured Him as the sinless and stainless One who knew no sin. The scapegoat pictured Him as One who took on Himself the sins of the world and bore them away from the face of God, taking our blame upon Him. And the lamb pictured the innocent dying for the guilty. Remember, when you read the Old Testament pages, the wonderful instructions about the sacrifices and offerings will take on new meaning if you remember that all of them speak of the Lord Jesus Christ.

2. But Our Text in Hebrews 13:11 Speaks of "the Bodies of Those Beasts, Whose Blood Is Brought Into the Sanctuary by the High Priest for Sin." That Must Refer to the Sin Offering Described in Leviticus 4:1–10

Let us read the story of that sin offering which has such blessed meaning to the Christian, which teaches us that we should go outside the gate with Jesus, bearing His reproach.

"And the Lord spake unto Moses, saying, Speak unto the children of Israel, saying, If a soul shall sin through ignorance against any of the commandments of the Lord concerning things which ought not to be done, and shall do against any of them: If the priest that is anointed do sin according to the sin of the people; then let him bring for his sin, which he hath sinned, a young bullock without blemish unto the Lord for a sin-offering. And he shall bring the bullock unto the door of the tabernacle of the congregation before the Lord; and shall lay his hand upon the bullock's head, and kill the bullock before the Lord. And the priest that is anointed shall take of the bullock's blood, and bring it to the tabernacle of the congregation: And the priest shall dip his finger in the blood, and sprinkle of the blood seven times before the Lord, before the vail of the sanctuary. And the priest shall put some of the blood upon the horns of the altar of sweet incense be-

fore the Lord, which is in the tabernacle of the congregation; and shall pour all the blood of the bullock at the bottom of the altar of the burnt-offering, which is at the door of the tabernacle of the congregation. And he shall take off from it all the fat of the bullock for the sin-offering; the fat that covereth the inwards, and all the fat that is upon the inwards, And the two kidneys, and the fat that is upon them, which is by the flanks, and the caul above the liver, with the kidneys, it shall he take away, As it was taken off from the bullock of the sacrifice of peace-offerings: and the priest shall burn them upon the altar of the burnt-offering."—Lev. 4:1–10.

In this case a young bullock was to be brought as the sacrifice. And since the bullock pictured the blameless Jesus, it must be "without blemish." The bullock was to be led to the door of the tabernacle of the congregation and there the priest would lay his hand upon the bullock's head and kill the bullock before the Lord. Then two things took place as an object lesson showing Christ's atoning death for sinners. First, the blood of the bullock offered in a certain way, then the fat of the bullock was offered. These pictured Christ's atoning work.

3. The Bullock's Blood Pictured Christ's Blood Shed on Calvary, Christ's Life Poured Out to Death for Sinners

I suppose that all the blood of the bullock was caught in a large basin. Then the priest dipped his finger in the blood and sprinkled the blood seven times before the vail of the sanctuary, that is, toward the Shekinah glory that dwelt over the mercy seat, beyond that vail. Then he put some of the blood upon the horns of the altar of sweet incense before the Lord. Everybody who ever approaches God must come on the basis of the blood of Jesus Christ which was shed. There is no entrance to God except by the blood. There can be no forgiveness, no fellowship, no redemption without the blood of Christ.

Next, the priest put some of the blood upon the horns of the altar of sweet incense before the Lord. That altar of sweet incense pictured prayers and praise ascending to God. But no prayer is acceptable to God which does not come in the merits of His Son Jesus Christ. No prayer or praise is acceptable to God except from the heart which has been cleansed by the blood. It certainly is not always necessary that we mention the blood of Christ in every prayer. But it is absolutely necessary that in our hearts we recognize the truth that everything we have from God we have, not on our own merits, but on the merits of the Lord Jesus Christ, our atoning Saviour. Be sure to remember the blood in your prayers and in your praises!

Then the priest took all the blood of the bullock and poured it out at the bottom of the altar of burnt-offering. In this we can see the dripping of the blood from the nail-torn hands extended on the cross. In this we can see the blood drops where the thorns pierced the Saviour's brow. We can see the blood dripping from the mutilated feet. We can see that crimson stream of blood that flowed from the side where the spear was driven to the very heart of the Son of God. The blood that made a pool dark and tragic in the dirt at the foot of the cross was pictured by the blood poured out at the foot of the big brazen altar every time the bullock for a sin offering was brought to the tabernacle, or later, to the temple.

Let us be sure to note that while this passage will have a rich and blessed meaning for the Christian and he can enter into part of the sacrifice that Christ makes, yet in this part the atoning blood pictures only the blood of Christ. The blood of a poor, sinful man could do no one any good. The bullock, in the poured-out blood, as in the blood sprinkled before the vail and the blood on the horns of the altar of incense, must picture the blood of Jesus Christ alone. Christ is the unique One, the only one who could atone for sin. Let us never, never forget this wonderful truth of the blood of Jesus Christ shed for sinners. God helping me, I will preach it as long as I have breath. When I get to Heaven I will join in the song of the redeemed who sing, "For thou wast slain, and hast redeemed us to God by thy blood out of every kindred, and tongue, and people, and nation" (Rev. 5:9).

I do not wonder that the Scripture speaks of His blood as "the precious blood of Christ" (I Pet. 1:19). The blood of Jesus was pure; and no other blood ever shed in this world since Adam sinned was ever pure!

Do not think that Abel was saved by the blood of the lamb he offered. Do not think that the Israelites had any peace with God on the merits of the blood of the passover lambs. No, no!

All the rivers of blood of animal sacrifices killed in Old Testament times simply pointed as object lessons to the coming Saviour. Their blood never washed away one sin, never put away the guilt of the conscience, never made any heart new. Only the blood of Jesus Christ could do that!

Once in Dallas, Texas, when I was pastor of the Galilean Baptist Church, the telephone in my study rang. When I answered, a woman in troubled voice said, "O Brother Rice, I'm at my wits' end! I'm in such trouble I don't know what to do!"

"What is it, Mrs. Hunter?" I asked.

"Pastor, you know that little Jackie, six years old, has had pneumonia. Now, after long weeks, his lungs have cleared. But he is so weak and frail. His blood is so thin. The doctor feels he cannot get well without a blood transfusion. I have a new baby and they will not let me give my blood. I have asked all the people I know, and no one wants to give blood for a transfusion. What shall I do? What shall I do?"

"I will take care of that," I answered. "Don't fret. We will have somebody at the hospital to have their blood typed at the hour appointed," I promised.

I found it difficult to get others to help. Everybody was busy. So in my own office I asked my brother, Bill, one of my secretaries, and in my home the Christian girl who helped Mrs. Rice. I went with them, and with the boy's father there were five of us. The doctor took samples of blood with a syringe from each of us. We were told that soon we would have a report and know which one, if any of us, would have the right type of blood for the transfusion.

"Doctor," I said, "I am glad to give blood for the transfusion if my blood will do, but I am promised to preach eighty miles away, at Bridgeport, Texas, tonight. So what you do, please do quickly and let me know."

The doctor agreed and I went to my home. As I sat at lunch the telephone rang. Of the five of us whose blood was tested, only my blood was sufficient and compatible. So I went to the hospital.

Little Jackie, the doctor, the nurses and Jackie's mother were waiting in the operating room when I went in. I pulled off my shirt and lay on an operating table. As the nurse prepared my arm for the needle through which the blood was to be drawn, little Jackie was rolled up beside me. A nurse put alcohol on his arm, too. The little fellow was frightened. He cried, "Mamma! What are they going to do to me? Mamma, make her quit!"

The mother knelt by the little fellow's side. "Now, Jackie, be a little man; don't break mother's heart. The doctor says that you need more blood to give you strength and to get you well. Daddy's blood wouldn't do. Miss Viola's blood wouldn't do. Miss Lillian's blood wouldn't do. Brother Bill's blood wouldn't do. Only Brother Rice's would do. So our pastor is going to give you some of his blood, and you will be strong and get well. Now be a brave little man for Mother."

The little fellow straightened up his face and there was hardly a whimper when the needle was put into the vein in his arm.

One nurse handled the transfusion equipment, the tube and measuring device between the two needles in my arm and in his arm.

"Twenty cubic centimeters, Doctor," she said. Another nurse wrote it down.

Again, "Twenty cubic centimeters, Doctor." The nurse recorded it.

After this the other nurse said, "Look at his cheeks becoming pink! His lips were so pale and now they are turning red again."

The doctor said, "His pulse is coming back good and strong. This little fellow is going to live and get well."

At last the nurse said, "That makes two hundred cubic centimeters, Doctor."

He said, "That is enough!" They drained the last blood from the tube into the little fellow's arm and as they were removing the needle and taping a bit of cotton over the place where the needle penetrated, the mother came to the little fellow's side and said to him, "Don't forget to thank Brother Rice. Wasn't he good to give you his blood when nobody else's blood would do?"

I thought to hurry away but the doctor insisted that I lie still for a bit, drink a glass of warm milk and be refreshed before I started to drive eighty miles to preach. As they pushed the wheeled cot through the door, little Jackie turned and waved to me and said, "Good-bye, Brother Rice! You're welcome."

I could not get the matter off my mind. That night I could preach on nothing but the precious blood, the only blood that would ever do anybody any good, the blood of Jesus Christ! I remember a woman with a sad and sin-marked face, with a baby in her arms. She tossed the baby to the woman next to her and trembling and weeping came to take Christ as her Saviour. Only the blood of Jesus Christ could make such a sinner clean and whole.

Oh, the precious blood of Christ! This blood of the bullock taken out and sprinkled before the vail and put on the horns of the altar of incense, and poured out before the big brazen altar pictured the blood of no one else but Jesus Christ Himself! Here in His atoning death the Lord Jesus walked alone. There will be many other things in which we can work with

Jesus. But when it came to paying for the sins of the world, Jesus Himself paid the debt alone!

This blessed teaching is given to us in Hebrews 10:11, 12:

"And every priest standeth daily ministering and offering oftentimes the same sacrifices, which can never take away sins: But this man, after he had offered one sacrifice for sins for ever, sat down on the right hand of God."

What can wash away my sin?
  Nothing but the blood of Jesus;
What can make me whole again?
  Nothing but the blood of Jesus.

Oh! precious is the flow
  That makes me white as snow;
No other fount I know,
  Nothing but the blood of Jesus.

And again, "Forasmuch as ye know that ye were not redeemed with corruptible things . . . But with the precious blood of Christ . . ." (I Pet. 1:18, 19).

4. The Bullock's Fat Pictured All Health and Prosperity and Riches Purchased for Us

Remember that, speaking of this sin-offering under discussion, Leviticus 4:8–10 tells us:

"And he [the priest] shall take off from it all the fat of the bullock for the sin-offering; the fat that covereth the inwards, and all the fat that is upon the inwards, And the two kidneys, and the fat that is upon them, which is by the flanks, and the caul above the liver, with the kidneys, it shall he take away, As it was taken off from the bullock of the sacrifice of peace-offerings: and the priest shall burn them upon the altar of the burnt-offering."

All the fat easily separated from the bullock's body was to be taken off the body and burned upon the big altar of burnt-offering. I remember how, as a boy, I used to help strip the leaf lard from butchered hogs and the extra fat from the inwards. So they were instructed to do with this bullock offered as a sin-offering. The fat was carefully removed and burned upon the altar.

That pictured that Jesus bought for us not only redemption from sin, but all prosperity and blessings which God has in store for those who come to Him through Jesus Christ. It is true that we have redemption through the blood of Christ. But we have far more than that. We are made sons of God. We are made partakers of all heavenly blessings in Christ Jesus. We are to inherit the New Jerusalem, and to inherit with Christ the transformed earth. We are not only kept out of Hell, but we have everlasting life. We will have glorified and perfected bodies forever! Oh, the unsearchable riches which God has prepared for those who love Him! And such other blessings, all the goodness and health and prosperity and riches that a Christian will ever have, were purchased for us in the atoning death of Jesus Christ! Not only did Christ offer redeeming blood for our sins; He offered His perfect life to take the place of our sinful ones. He offered His reputation for our disrepute. He offered His standing as a Son to us who were strangers and aliens. For His dear name's sake we are called sons. We are taken into the family of God! We call Him "our Father"! We are not only forgiven sinners; we are kings and priests unto God and we will reign with Christ on the earth!

We Christians are invited to go outside the gate and partake of the sacrifice which was never eaten by priests and Levites. We are to be partakers with Christ in His reproach. But let us never forget that we are not earning our blessings. We cannot buy our salvation. We have never deserved the honors, the joys, the blessings which are poured out without measure along with salvation. Christ on the cross did not only save us from Hell but He bought us every blessing that falls from the hand of God.

In us by nature there is nothing but poverty, decay, and sin. We ought to say as did Paul, "In me (that is, in my flesh,) dwelleth no good thing" (Rom. 7:18). The fat of the bullock burned on the altar of burnt-offering pictured the goodness, righteousness, health, prosperity, and riches of the dear Saviour, offered to us doomed sinners for whom He died.

II. The Sacrifice Picturing Jesus As the Despised and Rejected Saviour

Let us go back to our text. Hebrews 13:11, 12 tells us:

"For the bodies of those beasts, whose blood is brought into the sanctuary by the high priest for sin, are burned without the camp. Wherefore Jesus also, that he might sanctify the people with his own blood, suffered without the gate."

This passage is not primarily about the atonement of Christ on the cross. The pouring out of the blood, the burning of the fat, wonderful and blessed truths, are not the main point of discussion in our text in the epistle to the Hebrews. The Scripture here does not deal particularly with the blood of a bullock nor its fat, but with the body, after the blood and fat are removed.

I take up the story again in Leviticus 4. We considered the first ten verses telling how the blood was taken and sprinkled before the vail and put on the horns of the altar of incense, and poured out at the altar of burnt-offering: and how the fat of the bullock was taken away and burned on that same altar. But now read the following verses:

"And the skin of the bullock, and all his flesh, with his head, and with his legs, and his inwards, and his dung, Even the whole bullock shall he carry forth without the camp unto a clean place, where the ashes are poured out, and burn him on the wood with fire: where the ashes are poured out shall he be burnt."—Lev. 4:11, 12.

What does this picture teach us? The preceding verses have already made clear that the blood of Christ was offered to pay for our souls and how the goodness and riches of Christ were offered for our poverty. But these verses teach us a surprising fact. Let us consider it.

1. Christ Is Still Hated and Rejected by Most of the World

When God sent His Son, the Lord Jesus, into the world, did the whole world receive Him gladly with praises? No, there was no room for Him in the inn. He was born in a stable and made His bed in a manger! When He was a baby, Herod tried to kill Him. He grew up in direst poverty. When Jesus began to preach His wonderful gospel and offer Himself as God's Son and Messiah, did people love Him, trust Him, receive Him, and follow Him? No, they hated Him. The religious leaders arrested Him, accused Him falsely and with bribed witnesses they condemned Him to die. They had Him nailed to a Roman cross. They mocked Him while He hanged there in agony and died.

Now that the gospel has been carried to all the world, how do men receive it? It seems surely men everywhere would love such a Saviour, would believe such a gospel, would obey such a message. Instead, Christ is despised. The gospel is rejected. The Bible is criticized. We had as well face it; this world is no friend of Jesus Christ. As Charles Wesley put it, "Is this vile world a friend to grace, to help me on to God?" No, Christ is now the rejected Saviour. He is, as was prophesied, "despised and rejected of men" (Isa. 53:3). If Jesus Christ were here today, men, just as wickedly as those who knew Him and rejected Him, would hate Him and kill Him, as before, if they could.

So the Old Testament Scriptures, divinely inspired with the very wisdom of God, pictured the Saviour as rejected. So that bullock, offered as a sin-offering, was carried, minus the blood and fat, outside the gate of the city there in a clean place, a place of ashes, where it was burned. And that pictured the Lord Jesus being led out the way of sorrows through the gate of Jerusalem, to the hill called Calvary, and there nailed to a Roman cross and dying for the sins of the world. And the Lord Jesus is still outside the gate. He is still despised and rejected. This world still crucifies the Son of God afresh and puts Him to an open shame.

This doctrine is not popular. Many church men like to think that they are slowly making the world better. They like to think that man is inherently good, and if we pass enough laws, found enough schools, organize enough labor unions, and do away with race discrimination, that little by little man will turn out to be the very un-fallen son of God. Men like to think that man is naturally good, and with an opportunity he will turn out well. A great Methodist writer insists that all children are by nature the children of God and do not need to be converted or born again. Many churches who perhaps have something like this in mind, take little children into the church, and take unconverted men into the church in hope that the church can make them good Christians, with its good environment, and its "means of grace."

Postmillennialists long contended that this world would have its millennium of righteousness and peace before the second coming of Christ. But postmillennialists have grown discouraged and have become very rare. Now the same kind of men have given up hope of a millennium. Yet they keep on trying to repair this broken-down old world which God has said is headed for ruin.

I think Christians should do all they can to improve society. Christians should help make good laws, should help promote good education, civic enterprises. But we had as well face the inevitable fact; this world is headed for judgment. Men are a degenerate, fallen race. "The heart is deceitful above all things, and desperately wicked: who can know it?" (Jer. 17:9).

Do you think this world loves Jesus Christ? The world has

its Christmas, but it is a Christmas of lies about Santa Claus, drunkenness, revelry, and commercialism. It is not, on the part of the unsaved world and nominal Christians, a Christian Christmas. This world has its Easter. It is a very convenient time to sell new hats and suits. And Lent, with a very slight self-sacrifice and a good deal of religious formalism, pleases self-righteous people. But Easter time to the world and to nominal Christians is not a Christian Easter, glorying in the resurrection of Christ and in the resurrection that born-again Christians will have by virtue of His death and resurrection.

It is true that our cities are cluttered with church buildings. But Christ Himself is left out of many of them. Sometimes His place is taken by statues and by robed priests and by candles and ceremonies. Sometimes His place is taken by a Christ-denying, Bible-rejecting modernism. Sometimes the formalism of stained-glass windows and robed choirs and music during prayer take the place of a living Christ.

This world has rejected Jesus Christ! Most of the people in the world are against Him, not for Him! And Christ now does not have the place of an accepted and loved King, loyally obeyed. He has not the place of a Saviour and God worshipped and served with all the heart. No, Christ Jesus has the place of a rejected Saviour. And even among most Christians He has the place of Saviour without the place of Lord. He does not have the honor and the obedience which is His due. He is not on the throne in this world but on the cross. Even in the lives of most Christians He has still a place of reproach.

So when you think about Christ, you must think of Him as being still outside the gate of Jerusalem, not in the temple recognized as God and not on the throne obeyed as King. When you think about Christ, you must think about Him as displeasing the learned and the famous and the important people in this world. Men generally pay lip service to Christ but do not love Him, do not follow Him, do not wholeheartedly obey Him. Christ is outside the gate. He bears the reproach of crucifixion with thieves. He bears a crown of thorns on His head. There are marks of nails in His hands and in His feet. In His side is the huge scar of the spear! In the heart of Jesus which poured out all its blood for sinners there is the anguish of unrequited love. Those who would go with Jesus will need to go outside the gate, away from the center of things, away from the favor of this world, and go to the place of reproach.

III. But This Sacrifice Can Represent Christians

Now we come to the heart of the meaning of the text. The blood of the bullock did not picture us; it pictured Christ alone. The fat of the bullock, burnt on the altar, did not picture our goodness, our health, our wealth. It pictured the goodness, riches and wealth of Jesus Christ, offered to us and purchased for us. He became poor that we might be rich.

The body of this bullock also, with his head, his legs, his inwards, his dung, and his skin, carried outside the gate to a clean place and burned, pictured Jesus. But it may also picture us. Thank God!

1. After Salvation, Christians Are One With Christ

Now that Christ has died for me, now that I have accepted His atoning blood to pay for my sins, thank God, I can be like Jesus, can follow Jesus, can go where He goes, can be counted one with Christ! This is one of the richest and most heartening truths in the Word of God.

It is foolish to ask a lost man to live the Christ life. How can a man live a Christian life when he does not have a Christian heart? How can a man who is a child of the Devil live as if he were a child of God? But, thank God, now that I am born of God, I enter into a blood relationship to Jesus Christ. We are told that the very reason and purpose of God's foreknowledge and predestination is that all of us who trust in

Jesus should be "conformed to the image of his Son." His purpose is "that He [Jesus] might be the firstborn among many brethren" (Rom. 8:29).

Are we really sons of God and brothers of Jesus? That is what the Scripture says! Again the same teaching is given elsewhere. "For both he that sanctifieth and they who are sanctified are all of one: for which cause he is not ashamed to call them brethren" (Heb. 2:11).

I am a brother of Jesus Christ. He was born into this world by miraculous conception, wrought by the Holy Spirit. I had a human father in my first birth, but when I was born again, in the new birth I was conceived of the Holy Ghost and a similar miracle made me a child of God!

I think we should notice that Hebrews (chapter 2, verse 11) talks about Christ who sanctifies us and says that we and He "are all of one," and that He is not ashamed to call us brethren, and then soon thereafter we are called "brethren" again. Hebrews 3:1 says, "Wherefore, holy brethren, partakers of the heavenly calling, consider the Apostle and High Priest of our profession, Christ Jesus." I think that Hebrews 3:1 refers back to Hebrews 2:11 and that by divine inspiration all of us here are addressed as holy brethren, sanctified by Jesus Christ, and so partakers of the holy calling to be sons of God and brethren of Christ.

Remember that Jesus is the second Adam. As Adam is the head of all our fallen race, so Christ is the head of the new race, created by the new birth.

Remember that Jesus chose to be called "Son of man." Oh, yes, He was and is the Son of God, deity incarnate. And all of us might well call Him what doubting Thomas called Him, when his doubts about the risen Saviour were gone forever—"My Lord and my God!" (John 20:28). But Jesus emphasized the fact that He was a man. He was born of a woman. He made Himself one of our race. And, thank God, now Jesus and we "are all of one."

It is God's plan that we shall be "conformed to the image

of his Son." And we have this startling statement in Holy Writ that "as he is, so are we in this world" (I John 4:17).

At Christ's coming (O glorious event!) He will "change our vile body . . . like unto his glorious body" (Phil. 3:21).

Even the psalmist knew this in Old Testament times. He said, "I shall be satisfied, when I awake, with thy likeness" (Psa. 17:15). Oh, yes, Christians are identified with Christ.

The ordinances of the church are meant to picture this truth, that one who comes to Christ enters into His life and death. Baptism pictures that the believer has become theoretically dead to sin, no longer under the domination of sin. A believer is buried to indicate that he is dead and his life hid in God. He is raised from the watery grave to picture the resurrection of Christ and his own future resurrection. And all who were baptized were baptized with reference to the death of Christ and pointing to His death and resurrection. Christians are to be partakers of Christ's death and partakers of His resurrected power. In the Lord's Supper, too, the Christian takes the bread and the cup in memory of Christ's death and sufferings for us. Surely, also, Christians mean, in the Lord's Supper, to partake of Christ's life, of His death, and of His power.

2. Christians Should Do the Same Work Jesus Did

When Jesus had risen from the dead, He breathed on His disciples and said, "As my Father hath sent me, even so send I you" (John 20:21). Christians are to do the very work of Jesus Christ! Again He told the disciples assembled in the upper room, "He that believeth on me, the works that I do shall he do also; and greater works than these shall he do; because I go unto my Father" (John 14:12).

We are to have the same attitude that Jesus had. We are commanded, "Let this mind be in you, which was also in Christ Jesus" (Phil. 2:5).

Jesus called His disciples and said to them, "Follow me, and I will make you fishers of men" (Matt. 4:19). We, too, are to follow Jesus, to live like Jesus, to have His power, preach His gospel.

I tremble when I think of doing the very work that Jesus would do if He were here; but that is what God tells me to do. And it is a comfort to me to know that if Jesus were to come to a service where I was scheduled to preach, and if I should give up the pulpit and with holy tears urge Him to preach to the people, the Lord Jesus might well borrow my Bible. Certainly He would preach from the same blessed Word of God as I use! Jesus and I are in the same blessed business! Christians are to do the very same work that Jesus did here on earth. We have the same heavenly Father and, thank God, we poor creatures will awake in His likeness, and our bodies will be like His glorious body.

Jesus said, "I am the light of the world" (John 8:12). He also said, "Ye are the light of the world" (Matt. 5:14). We have a blessed part in Christ's salvation for sinners. Christ alone suffered on Calvary to pay for sin, but we may join in His concern of soul for sinners. We may weep with Him, work with Him, and be in some sense saviours with Him. Paul said, "I . . . fill up that which is behind of the afflictions of Christ in my flesh for his body's sake, which is the church" (Col. 1:23, 24).

3. So All Good Christians Should Be Partakers of the Sufferings and the Reproach of Christ

Christians ought to suffer hardship, ought to be persecuted. If they follow the Lord Jesus closely enough, they will be persecuted. They will have reproach. This is a clear doctrine of the Bible, frequently occurring in the Scriptures. The Lord Jesus in the Beatitudes said:

"Blessed be ye poor: for your's is the kingdom of God. Blessed are ye that hunger now: for ye shall be filled. Blessed are ye that weep now: for ye shall laugh."—Luke 6:20, 21.

In other words, this life is not the time for reaping, but

for sowing. This life is not the time for reigning, but for suffering. This is not the time for crowns, but for crosses. Then the Saviour continued:

"Blessed are ye, when men shall hate you, and when they shall separate you from their company, and shall reproach you, and cast out your name as evil, for the Son of man's sake. Rejoice ye in that day, and leap for joy: for, behold, your reward is great in heaven: for in the like manner did their fathers unto the prophets."—Luke 6:22, 23.

And again,

"Woe unto you, when all men shall speak well of you! for so did their fathers to the false prophets."—Luke 6:26.

What should a Christian expect in this world? He should expect hate from the world instead of love. He should expect to be separated from men instead of taken to their bosoms. He should expect to be reproached, to be cast out as evil for Jesus' sake. And how should the Christian feel about it? He should rejoice and leap for joy. He should know that he will have great reward in Heaven. He should know that good men of God in all time past have suffered in that way. Christians, if they be true to Christ, if they rightly exemplify Spirit-filled Christianity, will have the reproach of Christ upon them.

But what a curse is to come upon Christians who are not true to Christ; who please the world instead of their Master! To them Jesus said,

"Woe unto you, when all men shall speak well of you! for so did their fathers to the false prophets."—Luke 6:26.

No Christian ought ever allow himself to be criticized because he doesn't pay honest debts, because he is unkind, because he is guilty of crime or sin or lack of love. But a Christian who is really true to Christ will be treated, as were the prophets of old, with scorn and reproach and persecution. This is the clear teaching of the Lord Jesus Himself, a pattern for Christians during this whole age.

If the dear Lord Jesus had only a few hours with His disciples before He would be taken away and crucified, what would He say to them? We know what He said, at least in part. John, chapters 13 to 16, tells what Jesus said to the disciples in the precious crowded hours in the upper room before Jesus went to the Garden of Gethsemane, and on the road there. Jesus urged the disciples to be of good cheer, to have the peace of God, to be filled with the Spirit. He told them to be fruitful branches abiding in Christ and bearing fruit. He told them to love one another. One of the things that Jesus finally told them was that they must expect persecution:

"If the world hate you, ye know that it hated me before it hated you. If ye were of the world, the world would love his own: but because ye are not of the world, but I have chosen you out of the world, therefore the world hateth you. Remember the word that I said unto you, The servant is not greater than his lord. If they have persecuted me, they will also persecute you; if they have kept my saying, they will keep your's also. But all these things will they do unto you for my name's sake, because they know not him that sent me."—John 15:18–21.

Dear Christian reader, are you better than the Saviour? Is the servant any better than his lord? What kind of Christians are we, who are so well-loved and respected, when the Lord Jesus was hated and murdered?

This is the standard for good Christians throughout the Bible. Read again in Hebrews 11 the story of the heroes of the faith and remember that Abraham, the rich man, dwelt in tents and was a sojourner without a home in the land which God had promised eventually to give to him and his seed forever. Remember Moses who took on himself the reproach of a race of slaves and left Pharaoh's palace and refused to be called the son of Pharaoh's daughter. Remember that we are told about how these great Christians accepted suffering and persecution:

"And others were tortured, not accepting deliverance; that they might obtain a better resurrection: And others had trial of cruel mockings and scourgings, yea, moreover of bonds and imprisonment: They were stoned, they were sawn asunder, were tempted, were slain with the sword: they wandered about in sheepskins and goatskins; being destitute, afflicted, tormented; (Of whom the world was not worthy:) they wandered in deserts, and in mountains, and in dens and caves of the earth. And these all, having obtained a good report through faith, received not the promise."—Heb. 11:35b–39.

And these saints and martyrs who were outcasts, who lived in caves, who dressed in sheepskins and goatskins, who were destitute, afflicted, tormented, are very holy examples held up to Christians. God give us grace to pattern our lives after theirs!

Paul the apostle knew this blessed teaching and taught it and exemplified it, by the Holy Spirit's help. He wrote to Timothy, "Yea, and all that will live godly in Christ Jesus shall suffer persecution" (II Tim. 3:12). Paul tells us that he had left everything with the intent "that I may know him, and the power of his resurrection, and the fellowship of his sufferings, being made conformable unto his death" (Phil. 3:10). Paul had left some things, to be converted. But then for long years he continued to be persecuted, hounded, beaten, imprisoned, all for the dear name of the Saviour whom he loved and served. He wanted to know Christ not only in salvation, but in power, the power of the resurrected Christ. He wanted to know the Lord Jesus not only in the joy of forgiveness of sin, but in the fellowship of sufferings. He wanted his life to be "made conformable unto his death." Paul could say, therefore, "I die daily" (I Cor. 15:31). Paul set out to prove himself a good minister of the Lord Jesus. How? Not so much with eloquence of language as with eloquence in deeds. Along with a list of other values inherent in a good minister of Jesus Christ, there is the continual scarlet thread of suffering for Jesus. Paul said:

> *"But in all things approving ourselves as the ministers of God, in much patience, in afflictions, in necessities, in distresses, In stripes, in imprisonments, in tumults, in labours, in watchings, in fastings; By pureness, by knowledge, by longsuffering, by kindness, by the Holy Ghost, by love unfeigned, By the word of truth, by the power of God, by the armour of righteousness on the right hand and on the left, By honour and dishonour, by evil report and good report: as deceivers, and yet true; As unknown, and yet well known; as dying, and, behold, we live; as chastened, and not killed; As sorrowful, yet alway rejoicing; as poor, yet making many rich; as having nothing, and yet possessing all things."*—II Cor. 6:4–10.

In the examination of my heart, long ago, I went through this list and checked to find out if I were a good minister of Jesus. I have not been in prison. I have not had stripes on my back for preaching the gospel; but oh, I have longed to be counted worthy to suffer for Christ's sake.

What are these proofs of a good minister of Jesus Christ? They are "in afflictions, in necessities, in distresses, in stripes, in imprisonments, in tumults . . ." It is by honor, but also by dishonor. It is by evil report as well as by good report. It is by being called a deceiver, when one brings the only certain truth there is in this world. It is by being unknown, and dying, and chastened, yet always protected and alive in Christ. It is by being in sorrow, yet always rejoicing; by being poor while we make others rich in eternal riches. It is by having nothing while others around us do not labor as hard, and have luxuries—and yet with the certainty that God and Christ are ours and all eternity and every good thing!

Are you a good servant of Jesus Christ, proven by suffering, afflictions, by distress, by dishonor, by chastening, by being killed instead of living?

I long ago resolved that, God helping me, I would not meet the Lord Jesus and have to tell Him that I had never suffered for Him. How I pity all the people who never lost a dollar, never lost a night's sleep, never missed a meal, never did without a new car, never lost a job, never were called nuts or fools or holy rollers or fanatics for Jesus Christ's sake! A Christian ought to be able and willing to suffer the reproach of Christ.

IV. What It Means for a Christian to Bear the Reproach of Christ

Yes, we have a sacrifice which they have no right to eat which served the tabernacle. For we are told that "the bodies of those beasts, whose blood is brought into the sanctuary by the high priest for sin, are burned without the camp." And let us turn back again and see what was involved in the body of that beast carried outside the camp.

In Leviticus 4:12 we read:

"Even the whole bullock shall he carry forth without the camp unto a clean place, where the ashes are poured out, and burn him on the wood with fire: where the ashes are poured out shall he be burnt."

1. The Body of the Bullock Was Carried to a Clean Place. So Christians, to Have the Reproach of Christ, Must Live Cleanly

The Lord Jesus is different from the world. We should be different from the world also. I do not have space here to take up all the questions of smoking, even moderate drinking, dirty picture shows, promiscuous necking and petting, the dance, and such evils. But I think that surely any Christian ought to know that a Christian should be different. I believe a Christian ought not to smell like a lost sinner, because he ought not to have the same habits. I believe that a Christian ought not to take the same bloody oaths which unsaved people banded together in the lodges take. I believe that a Christian ought not to look upon the same lewd films which fascinate the unsaved man and woman and color their lives for evil. The Christian should be different.

I wonder, is your life in a clean place so that you can have fellowship with the Lord Jesus, can know His power, can take upon you His reproach?

2. The Christian Must Live in the Place of Ashes, if He Would Bear the Reproach of Christ

The place outside the gate where the body of the bullock was taken was the place "where the ashes are poured out." The burning of the bodies of the bullocks would produce more ashes all the time. The Christian should live in the place of ashes!

Are there any ashes in your life? Have you burned up dream castles? Have you laid on the fire of God's altar a sacrifice of things dearest to your heart?

I was a college teacher and I loved to teach. I did graduate work briefly in the University of Chicago and had a contract for another year for teaching. I had dreamed that I would soon become a college president and who knows, perhaps then a senator, a famous author and more—any vigorous young man can dream! But one day in Chicago in the Pacific Garden Mission I put my arms around a drunken bum and won him to Christ. There were many tears, there were holy confessions, there was an abandon of surrender and faith in Christ. And the man was miraculously transformed.

I got up from my knees beside this poor, dirty, unshaven, but now converted bum, and found that all my ambitions for college teaching were gone! I wanted nothing better than to win souls and to have welling up in my heart continually the glad joy I felt at that moment. I looked through the vista of future years and saw the time when "they that be wise shall shine as the brightness of the firmament; and they that turn many to righteousness as the stars for ever and ever" (Dan. 12:3). I gave up my graduate work, gave up my contract, started revival work, then entered the seminary for ministerial training.

What I did then, I have since done a hundred times, a thousand times. I have said good-by to good friends for Jesus' sake. I have laid on the altar the dearest things a man can know in this world, save the love of God and the presence of the Holy Spirit, and eternal blessings. I have loved those who did not love me. I have helped those who did not thank me. I have through the long years willingly paid whatever price God would help me pay to help bring back revivals. I have been unknown when I could be known. I have been despised when I could have been honored.

No man can be of much use to Christ who is not willing to set the match to possessions, careers, and loves of his life. Abraham left Ur of the Chaldees, and home. Ruth said good-by to her Moabite kinspeople and went with Naomi to the land of the true God where she was a stranger. One day Jesus walked by the Sea of Galilee and called two brothers, Peter and Andrew, promising to make them fishers of men, "and they straightway left their nets, and followed him" (Matt. 4:20). He saw other brothers, James and John, and called them "and they immediately left the ship and their father, and followed him" (Matt. 4:22). It may have been harder to leave their father than the ship, but the ship and father and nets and career were all laid on the altar of sacrifice and the fire was lighted. They lived in the place of ashes.

Levi or Matthew was a publican, a prosperous tax collector, but when he heard Jesus say, "Follow me," then, we are told, "he left all, rose up, and followed him" (Luke 5:27, 28). That is what God calls every Christian to do—simply to "leave all." Whatever it is, put it on the altar! I loved fine horses. Riding was almost as natural with me as walking, but I bade them good-by to preach.

C. T. Studd gave up a fortune, and went to be a missionary in China. Later he gave up his sick wife and left her, not to see her for years. After signing away all his money and giving up the joy of his family, eventually Studd could say, "I honestly do not know anything else I can give up to Jesus Christ." But, in fact, the dear Lord insists that life itself shall be laid on the altar. We should be ready to live or die. "If any man will come after me, let him deny himself, and take up his cross daily, and follow me" (Luke 9:23). Again Jesus said, "If any man come to me, and hate not his father, and mother, and wife, and children, and brethren, and sisters, yea, and his own life also, he cannot be my disciple. And whosoever doth not bear his cross, and come after me, cannot be my disciple" (Luke 14:26, 27). God wants the fire set to personal loves, personal ambitions and personal possessions. He wants you to come to the place of ashes. In fact, Jesus said plainly, "So likewise, whosoever he be of you that forsaketh not all that he hath, he cannot be my disciple" (Luke 14:33). You may be a child of God and know Jesus as your Saviour without suffering for Him, without forsaking things for Him. But you cannot be His disciple, His learner; you cannot walk in His footsteps, you cannot follow Him truly, except by forsaking all and going outside the gate unto Him, and bearing His reproach.

Is it too much to ask that we should give up things for the Lord Jesus, when He has given up so much for us?

> I gave My life for thee,
> My precious blood I shed,
> That thou might'st ransomed be,
> And quickened from the dead;
> I gave, I gave My life for thee,
> What hast thou given for Me?
>
> My Father's house of light,
> My glory-circled throne

I left for earthly night,
  For wanderings sad and lone;
I left, I left it all for thee,
Hast thou left aught for Me?

I suffered much for thee,
  More than thy tongue can tell,
Of bitterest agony,
  To rescue thee from Hell;
I've borne, I've borne it all for thee,
What hast thou borne for Me?

And I have brought to thee,
  Down from My home above,
Salvation full and free,
  My pardon and My love;
I bring, I bring rich gifts to thee,
What hast thou brought to Me?

How can you answer the question by Frances R. Havergal in the hymn above? How could you satisfy Jesus Christ without laying everything on the altar for Him, and taking on you His reproach?

To be sure, there are many daily joys for a Christian. A Christian father enjoys his baby more than a lost man, I suppose. A Christian should enjoy his food, should enjoy blessings to make his heart happy every day. A Christian should know better the joys of a Christian family life. But at the same time, everything the Christian has should be laid on the altar, offered to God with sincere heart. For the Christian it should make no matter, to live or die, just so he is in the very place where God wants him. Is your life lived in the place of ashes?

3. The Reproach Pictures the Bad Odor, the Reproach Which Goes With the Best Christianity

Can you imagine how it smelled in that place where the carcasses of the sin-offerings were burned? Think of the hair, the hide, the horns, the hoofs, the bones burning, with the dung and flesh. And remember that there were many sin-offerings. I have no doubt that the fires were kept burning there continually. I know how that smelled, for I lived in Fort Worth, Texas, long ago and when the wind was right we could smell, six miles away, the burning of dung and refuse outside the big packing plants on the north side. Surely that odor pictures part of the reproach that is on Christians.

An evangelist came to Dallas, Texas, to hold revival services in the big tabernacle of what is now the Galilean Baptist Church. The evangelist, after trying to get the cooperation of a good many other churches, said to me indignantly, "There is a stink on this place! There is a reproach on this tabernacle!"

And there was. In that tabernacle we had seen hundreds saved, including drunkards, convicts, harlots and bums, as well as many respectable citizens. But many of the worldly Christians and pastors did not like the tabernacle. We preached hard against sin. Churches full of lodge members, churches where the Sunday School teachers attended picture shows and played bridge, where the pastors and deacons were members of lodges and smoked cigarettes, did not like that place. I preached hard against sin, and so the people said that we were fanatics. In the big popular church two blocks away, with thousands of members, the pastor smoked cigars and his daughter was an artist's model. In the pastor's meeting which I sometimes attended one-half of the pastors smoked cigars and cigarettes during the session of the ministers' meeting. You may be sure I was not very grateful for their example. The blessing of God was on our church. In one six months' period we counted 1,005 people who claimed to trust Christ as Saviour or who returned from backsliding sin. I suppose I baptized a hundred drunkards among hundreds of other converts taken into the church. But to one who does not win very many souls the evangelist seems "sensational" and "too emotional." To the person who does not believe that Christ will come again, as He said, the premillennialist, rejoicing in the blessed hope, is counted like Jehovah's Witnesses and other false cults. To those who care more for the "learning" of the big universities, one who believes in the verbal inspiration of the Bible and the scientific accuracy and historical correctness of the Word of God, is counted unscientific and, perhaps, very ignorant!

Do you live in the place of burning?

Not long ago at our home the water boiled away from a saucepan of cooking beans. The pot was burned black inside. The smoke billowed up and filled the whole house. The hideous smell seemed to enter every cranny and corner. We worked and worked to ventilate the house in mid-winter to try to get rid of the stink. I tell you, dear Christian, if your life is lived in the place of burning, constantly on the altar, there will be a stink that the world does not like.

I think that the bloody sin-offering bullock, burned outside the gate, may have been the beginning of the tradition about the Valley of Hinnom, later called Gehenna, a type of Hell, and even the word used for Hell sometimes in the New Testament. Here the carcasses were burning always. The bodies of criminals were cast out into the Valley of Hinnom, and the bodies of dead animals were piled there, too. Maggots and fire together destroyed the offal. Very properly that desolate and dreadful place became a type of Hell. But I remind you that the Lord Jesus tasted death for every man. He died between two thieves. He suffered the tortures of the damned. Even now He is, like Paul, the off-scouring of the world. In that sense Christians should suffer some of what wicked people deserve, in order to keep people out of Hell. Is your life a place of burning? Do you live in the place of reproach for Jesus' sake?

4. But This Place Outside the Gate, Where We Are to Go, Is, Thank God, a Place in the Presence of Jesus

Going unto Him! I would rather go to Jesus outside the gate than to live in the city, in the throng, in the palace, even on the throne, with anybody else or everybody else in the world!

Jessie Brown Pounds has said so well,

> Anywhere with Jesus I can safely go;
> Anywhere He leads me in this world below;
> Anywhere without Him dearest joys would fade;
> Anywhere with Jesus I am not afraid.
> Anywhere, anywhere! Fear I cannot know;
> Anywhere with Jesus I can safely go.

Here is our recompense. If we take the reproach of Christ we can have the power of Christ and the joy of His blessed presence.

Remember that it was to know Christ and the power of His resurrection and the fellowship of His suffering, even being made conformable to His death, that Paul suffered the loss of all things and counted them but dung.

Now, I want to tell you something wonderful that I found in the study of that sin-offering bullock, discussed in Leviticus 4:1–12. Please open your Bible and look carefully to see what I will now show you in the Word of God. In the first three chapters of Leviticus priests are mentioned again and again. The Scripture speaks of "the priests, Aaron's sons," and again "the sons of Aaron the priest" and "the priest," etc. Some twenty-two times in those three chapters the priests are mentioned, as I have described. But when we enter into the fourth chapter, describing the sin offering which is to be a special lesson for the separated, Spirit-filled Christians, then an added word is given about priests. Leviticus 4:3 says, "If *the priest that is anointed* do sin. . . ."

And in verse 5 the Scripture says, "And *the priest that is anointed* shall take of the bullock's blood. . . ." And again, in verse 16, which we did not discuss, but speaking of the sin offering for the whole congregation, the Scripture says, "And *the priest that is anointed* shall bring of the bullock's blood. . . ."

We know that priests in the Old Testament are types of Christians. Christians "shall be priests of God and of Christ"

(Rev. 20:6). "And hast made us unto our God kings and priests: and we shall reign on the earth" (Rev. 5:10). First Peter 2:5 says that we are "an holy priesthood." Priests in the Old Testament picture Christians. But here are some "anointed" priests. And they surely must picture Spirit-filled Christians. Not every Christian is a Spirit-filled Christian. Not every person who has salvation has also soul-winning power. Every Christian has the indwelling of the Holy Spirit, but not every Christian has the fullness of the Spirit.

The lesson for us evidently is that only Spirit-filled Christians can really bear the reproach of Christ. The lesson in Leviticus 4:1–12 and in Hebrews 13:10–14 is for Spirit-filled Christians.

Remember that Jesus lived most of His first thirty years in Galilee at the little town of Nazareth. There He attended the synagogue and regularly read the Scriptures. He was blameless, sinless, perfect. He was a model young man, greatly respected. However, He had never preached a sermon, never healed the sick, never raised the dead, never won a soul, until He was thirty years old. Then He went to John the Baptist and was baptized in Jordan and there was filled with the Holy Spirit. Afterward He returned to Cana in Galilee and worked His first miracle at the wedding feast. Then Jesus came back to Nazareth where He was brought up, as the story is told in Luke 4:16–29. For the first time they heard Jesus when filled with the Holy Ghost. The One whom they had respected and honored, now they suddenly began to hate! A few moments after Jesus had told them He was filled with the Holy Spirit, according to the prophecy in Isaiah 61:1, 2, they tried to cast Him headlong from the cliff outside the city! When Jesus was filled with the Holy Spirit, He was then hated and persecuted.

Remember how Stephen, the first Christian martyr, was killed? It was because he was filled with the Holy Ghost. If we take on us the reproach of Christ, we have the fullness of the Spirit of God. And the persecution and the reproach which are here described as greatly to be desired, are for those who pay God's price for the fullness of His Spirit.

The soul winner, then, will be the one persecuted, slandered and abused. The one who enters into Christ's burden for sinners, into Christ's power of the Holy Spirit, will bear the reproach of Christ. But, praise God a thousand times, he will be where Jesus is! He will know the sweet presence of the dear Saviour.

Remember that Jesus said to His disciples who were to go in the power of the Holy Spirit and preach the gospel to every creature, "And lo, I am with you alway, even unto the end of the world" (Matt. 28:20).

5. "*Let Us Go Forth Therefore Unto Him Without the Camp . . .*"

It is clear that offering one's self for persecution, for ill report, for reproach, must be a matter of personal choice. You are not required to do this in order to be saved. Salvation is the free gift of God to all who come by simple faith and depend upon Jesus Christ. If a man should give his body to be burned that would not add one drop of merit to balance the ocean of his sins. Let us make no mistake; salvation is by the grace of God alone and Jesus Christ paid all that needed to be paid. When one offers to suffer for Jesus, to toil for Jesus, to be identified with the Lord Jesus whatever comes, that is the voluntary choice of one who is already a child of God, one already born again and certain for Heaven, by God's grace.

So the Scripture does not say, "You must go." But it says, "Let us go." In Romans 12:1, 2 Paul does not command but he entreats. "I beseech you therefore, brethren, by the mercies of God, that ye present your bodies a living sacrifice. . . ." The body must be *presented,* it is not *confiscated.* The service of the Christian soldier must be that of a volunteer, not of a draftee. We remember that Moses chose "rather to suffer affliction with the people of God, than to enjoy the pleasures of sin for a season" (Heb. 11:25). Knowing the eternal reward, Moses made the intelligent choice. He chose poverty instead of wealth. He chose the place of a rebellious slave instead of the place of a kingly son, in the sight of the Egyptians. But he chose the place of an obedient prophet of God instead of a fleshly worldling.

So I ask you to choose today. Will you, by choice, go outside the gate unto Jesus, and help bear His reproach? Will you enter into His burden, His concern over sinners, His condemnation of sin, His offering of Himself?

Nobody will compel you to do it. You will not do it unless you choose to do it. If you chose before, you will need to choose again and again. Choose then today to please God instead of men, to receive your honor in the next world instead of in this world.

The answer is made for us in the words of that grand old hymn:

Jesus, I my cross have taken,
  All to leave and follow Thee;
Destitute, despised, forsaken,
  Thou, from hence, my all shalt be:
Perish every fond ambition,
  All I've sought, and hoped, and known;
Yet how rich is my condition,
  God and heaven are still my own!

Let the world despise and leave me,
  They have left my Saviour, too;
Human hearts and looks deceive me;
  Thou art not, like man, untrue;
And, while Thou shalt smile upon me,
  God of wisdom, love, and might,
Foes may hate, and friends may shun me;
  Show Thy face, and all is bright.

Man may trouble and distress me,
  'Twill but drive me to Thy breast;

Life with trials hard may press me,
  Heaven will bring me sweeter rest.
O 'tis not in grief to harm me,
  While Thy love is left to me;
O 'twere not in joy to charm me,
  Were that joy unmixed with Thee.

Haste thee on from grace to glory,
  Armed by faith and winged by prayer;
Heaven's eternal day's before thee,
  God's own hand shall guide thee there.
Soon shall close thy earthly mission,
  Swift shall pass thy pilgrim days,
Hope shall change to glad fruition,
  Faith to sight, and prayer to praise.

—Henry F. Lyte

Now let us come back to the text with which we started.

"We have an altar, whereof they have no right to eat which serve the tabernacle. For the bodies of those beasts, whose blood is brought into the sanctuary by the high priest for sin, are burned without the camp. Wherefore Jesus also, that he might sanctify the people with his own blood, suffered without the gate. Let us go forth therefore unto him without the camp, bearing his reproach. For here have we no continuing city, but we seek one to come."—Heb. 13:10–14.

Are you living outside the gate with Jesus? Are you willing to bear the reproach of Christ?

3

Leaving All for Jesus

"And there went great multitudes with him: and he turned, and said unto them, If any man come to me, and hate not his father, and mother, and wife, and children, and brethren, and sisters, yea, and his own life also, he cannot be my disciple. And whosoever doth not bear his cross, and come after me, cannot be my disciple. For which of you, intending to build a tower, sitteth not down first, and counteth the cost, whether he have sufficient to finish it? Lest haply, after he hath laid the foundation, and is not able to finish it, all that behold it begin to mock him, Saying, This man began to build, and was not able to finish. Or what king, going to make war against another king, sitteth not down first, and consulteth whether he be able with ten thousand to meet him that cometh against him with twenty thousand? Or else, while the other is yet a great way off, he sendeth an ambassage, and desireth conditions of peace. So likewise, whosoever he be of you that forsaketh not all that he hath, he cannot be my disciple."—Luke 14:25–33.

TWO GREAT terms are used in the New Testament that should not be confused. One term is "saved." That refers to born-again people, people who have depended upon Jesus Christ for forgiveness and so are saved (Mark 16:6; Rom. 10:13; Acts 16:31, 32; Rom. 10:9, 10). But the other term, the one we discuss here, is the term "disciple." The two words do not mean the same thing. Everyone who depended upon Christ and trusted Him for salvation is saved, as many plain Scriptures declare. But the twelve apostles who left all to follow Jesus and went on themselves to indescribable suffering and then a martyr's death, are called disciples.

It is easy to be saved if one honestly turns from his sins and depends on Jesus Christ. That is an instantaneous matter. But the role of a disciple is a long and hard role. For to be a disciple means to be a learner under Jesus, to be one who follows Him, patterns after Him, and does the work of Jesus.

Every Christian ought to be a true disciple. But, sad to say, many Christians are not really disciples. They do not really learn of Jesus, do not follow Him, do not pattern after Him, and are not much like Him.

In the Scripture above we have the clear teaching of Jesus our Saviour and Lord as to what He requires for discipleship. He sums up the whole passage in these words, "So likewise, whosoever he be of you that forsaketh not all that he hath, he cannot be my disciple." It does not cost that much to be saved, to be a Christian. But it does cost that much to be a GOOD Christian.

Let us not think that Jesus here uses figurative language. For many of the men to whom He spoke literally did leave everything. Luke 5:10, 11 tells us:

"And so was also James, and John, the sons of Zebedee, which were partners with Simon. And Jesus said unto Simon, Fear not; from henceforth thou shalt catch men. And when they had brought their ships to land, they forsook all, and followed him."

Here Peter, Andrew, James and John literally left everything to follow Jesus. And they left them for good!

In the same chapter we find another man who left all to follow Jesus.

"And after these things he went forth, and saw a publican, named Levi, sitting at the receipt of custom: and he said unto him, Follow me. And he left all, rose up, and followed him." —Luke 5:27, 28.

They gave up business, ship, nets, jobs, income, father, loved ones; gave them up gladly and permanently for Jesus Christ. And we have good reason to believe that they literally, once-and-for-all, laid everything on the altar and said good-by to dearest wishes and plans and dreams and comforts to follow Jesus! They were disciples.

Many who read these words are Christians in the sense that you are born again, you are believers in Christ, and have been redeemed by trusting in Him. He has given you His Holy Spirit to live in your bodies, and has made you into new creatures. Yes, thousands who read this are Christians; but are you real disciples, according to the standard set up by the Saviour Himself? Then today take it to heart; here are the words of the dear Lord Jesus: "Whosoever he be of you that forsaketh not all that he hath, he cannot be my disciple."

I. What Christ Demands for Discipleship

I often feel sorry for people who work to make a living. Do not misunderstand me; I believe that good hard work is honorable and honored of God. But to work only for the things of this life, to pay for bread and meat, or house, or car, or clothes, or any other comforts or luxuries, seems so small and cheap now that I am accustomed to working to keep souls out of Hell for billions of years! How I thank God that the Lord "counted me worthy, putting me into the ministry," as Paul said!

I remember the time when I knelt by a drunken bum in the old Pacific Garden Mission in Chicago and showed him how to be saved. I saw the transformation in his face, the evidence of wonderful peace in his heart, and the change that took place in his life. And suddenly God gave me a glimpse of the eternal value of a soul, and of the joy of winning souls for Jesus and Heaven. That night I lost my taste for the college classroom where I had been teaching. I lost my ambition and my dreams to be a great educator. I saw at a glance that this was the grand labor, the labor with eternal rewards, the labor beside which no other toil or effort in the universe is comparable!

That only illustrates that as Jesus Christ is greater than all other leaders and teachers, and as His business is beyond compare greater than any other business, and as He Himself has paid such an infinite price beyond anything else that anybody else ever paid, then to follow Jesus and be His disciple costs more than to be a disciple of anybody else.

Consider the moral standards of infidels. Remember that Tom Paine was a patriot, writing tracts to help forward the cause of the American Revolution and the founding of the American Republic. He ranked near Washington and Jefferson in influence at one time. But his infidelity, his disbelief in the Bible and in Christ, set no great standards for him to live by. He died a poor, dirty, drunken wretch. It does not cost much to become a disciple of infidels.

A great doctor told how he was in Rush Medical School long years ago, before it became a part of the University of Chicago, when Robert Ingersoll, famous infidel, gave one of his lectures on "The Mistakes of Moses." Ingersoll said that there was no Hell. He scoffed at eternal retribution. He said that the Bible was a lie. And that great physician told how that night the other medical students went by droves to the bawdy houses. If there were no Hell, no judgment, if the Bible were not true, and if they were really descended from beasts, they might act like beasts. It does not cost much to be a disciple of infidels.

Modernists, that is, infidels in the church who do not believe that the Bible is God's infallible Word, who do not believe that Jesus Christ was the virgin-born Saviour, nor that His blood, shed on the cross, actually paid for man's sins, and do not believe that people can be regenerated only by faith in this personal Saviour, often seem to be such nice men. They often claim that modernists are better gentlemen, that they have more of "a Christian spirit" than fundamentalists have. What they really mean, whether they realize it or not, is that if one does not believe the Bible and does not accept Christ for all He claimed to be, they cannot set much of a standard. If Jesus Himself lied, and if the Bible is a book of myths and legends, and if there is no Hell and perhaps no Heaven, then we have no one to follow. No one can ever take the crown of deity from the dear head of Jesus Christ and still call people to sacrifice and suffering and the holiest endeavor and martyrdom. Such standards cannot be set by unbelievers. Unless one takes Jesus Christ as all He claimed to be, one can never hold up the standards which Jesus Himself set.

I would not leave all for a Saviour who was only a man like me. I would not forsake everything for One who was an illegitimate child of a fallen Jewish woman, One who claimed that He was one with God, but was actually either a maniac or a fool, or a charlatan and pretender. I say, I would not suffer the martyrdom, the blood, the sweat, the tears, the poverty, the physical torment, the ostracism and persecution that Bible Christians suffered for Jesus, if I did not believe that Jesus is all He claimed to be. And neither would anybody else.

But that is the reason that modernists always try to steal the churches and the schools and other Christian institutions which are built by the love and sacrifice and tears and labors of Bible believers. Modernists are like cuckoo birds which lay their eggs in the nests of other birds to have them hatched. Modernists themselves do not know the meaning of sacrifice. They themselves cannot hold up the standards of discipleship.

Be sure to get this thought; Jesus Christ, God in human flesh who gave Himself to suffer the torments of the damned, to keep people out of Hell, is Himself the mightiest of all teachers. To follow Him, to learn of Him, to pattern after Him, means to meet a standard that no other leader in history ever had a right to make. To be a good Christian is hard. It really costs to be a disciple of Jesus Christ. "Whosoever he be of you that forsaketh not all that he hath, he cannot be my disciple," Jesus said.

1. Jesus Demands Absolute Surrender and Unqualified Obedience

In the Great Commission the Lord Jesus said: "All power [or authority] is given unto me in heaven and in earth. Go ye therefore. . . ." Note that Jesus claims, without any embarrassment or hesitation, to have all the authority in this world! He claims the right to instant obedience of every soul who might ever live on this planet! He makes such claims as no one else ever has made or ever can make. And He has verified every claim!

Jesus does not simply ask that one give one day a week of his time. He demands all the days of all the weeks. Jesus does not require simply one-tenth of one's income, one dime out of every dollar. He requires all of the income. I do not mean that all the days ought to be spent in singing songs and hearing preaching. I do not mean that all the money ought to go into a church offering envelope. But I mean, honestly, without any exaggeration, that Jesus Christ demands absolute surrender of everything that comes into the life of one who would be a disciple.

The dear Lord Jesus does not ask that He would be next to a wife in the affection of the husband. He does not ask to be next to the father in the child's allegiance. He does not ask to be next to king or country in the patriot's heart. No, He asks to be dearer than a bride to the bridegroom, dearer than father and mother to the child, dearer than country to the citizen. Jesus asks for absolute surrender, unqualified obedience to every wish. In other words, He says, "Whosoever he be of you that forsaketh not all that he hath, he cannot be my disciple."

2. That Means That the Dear Lord Jesus Demands First Place, Absolutely First Place in the Life of Every Christian

If you would be a good Christian, then Christ must come

before everything else and everybody else. He must not only come before bad things, but come before good things. *Jesus demands absolutely first place.*

In the Old Testament offerings again and again people were required to bring "the firstlings of the flock." In Exodus 13:12, 13, 15, we are plainly told that the first-born of man and beast belong to God. The men were redeemed. Unclean beasts, not suitable for sacrifices, were redeemed or killed. But here is the divine law that the first-born of every beast and the first-born of man belongs to God. God requires first place! And even so it was with the crops of the field. The command was, "The first of the first-fruits of thy land thou shalt bring into the house of the Lord thy God." When Jesus Christ requires one to forsake all that He has in order to be His disciple, He is simply following the plain teaching of the Word of God, that God requires the very first and best.

A Jew was not allowed to bring anything maimed, or crippled, or wounded. Only the best will do for Jesus Christ.

In I Kings 17 we find that God commanded Elijah to go to the brook Cherith where he was fed by ravens. Then he was commanded to go to Zarephath and dwell there, and God said, "Behold, I have commanded a widow woman there to sustain thee." There he found near the city the widow gathering sticks. He asked her for a drink of water, and as she started to bring it, "he called to her, and said, Bring me, I pray thee, a morsel of bread in thine hand."

She replied that she had not a cake, but only a handful of meal in a barrel, and a little oil in a cruse, and she said, "Behold, I am gathering two sticks, that I may go in and dress it for me and my son, that we may eat it, and die."

Then Elijah made a strange request. It might appear selfish to the unbelieving. Actually it was a call to her to act in faith, giving God the first and trusting Him for supply. "And Elijah said unto her, Fear not; go and do as thou hast said: but make me thereof a little cake first, and bring it unto me, and after make for thee and for thy son." God's requirement was that the woman should first provide for the prophet of God, and then if any were left, for herself and her son.

To be sure God prospered the woman in her faith. That barrel of meal did not fail nor the cruse of oil, through long days. God multiplied the food which she had sanctified by putting God first. But this only illustrates the demand of Jesus Christ. As the widow left her little handful of meal and her bit of oil for the prophet, so God requires first place. Just as God required this widow to give an offering for the prophet of God before she took for herself and her son, so Jesus here means that "whosoever he be of you that forsaketh not all that he hath, he cannot be my disciple."

3. Obedience to Jesus Christ Takes Precedent Over All Earthly Ties

This means that Jesus comes before mother. Jesus comes before wife. Jesus comes before any other relative, any other loved one. Duty to Jesus Christ comes before any other duty. Loyalty to Christ comes before loyalty to government, loyalty to family, loyalty to any other authority. The command of Jesus is that the Christian who would be a disciple must literally "forsake all that he hath."

What a strange Scripture is the passage in Luke 14:25–33! Here Jesus said,

> *"If any man come to me, and hate not his father, and mother, and wife, and children, and brethren, and sisters, yea, and his own life also, he cannot be my disciple"* (vs. 26).

Must one, to be a good Christian, have malice in his heart against his dear mother who bore him, who fed him, clothed him, washed him, taught him and loved him? Someone has said that God could not be everywhere, so He made mothers. Well, that is not exactly true, because God can be everywhere, yet God does express His love to us by mother-love. But does being a good Christian turn that love into hate? Must one turn against his father, that prince and example, that demi-God of the home? Well, it is a startling saying of Jesus, that one cannot be His disciple without hating father, mother, wife, children, brothers and sisters. But there it is in the Bible.

Christ does not mean that a man is to have malice against his dear ones. The love of a Christian's heart for his own family—for wife, for children, for mother, brothers and sisters—does not curdle into animosity by the sweet influence of Christian grace in the heart! But there is a sense in which love for others is so superceded by the love of Christ that it becomes as nothing.

Love is a relative matter. I have seen a girl give her heart over to a young man so that she left father and mother and home to live in poverty with the young man she loved. Sometimes she did it so as to break the mother's heart and the father's. To such mothers and fathers it has often seemed that the child, brought up in their home, had learned to hate them and despise them, so cruelly did the child turn against the father and the mother. Actually what really happened was that the love for father and mother was still there, but it had been supplanted by a love so much stronger that it seemed as but hate.

So one can come to love Jesus Christ so that the wife will say to her husband, "Since you have gotten so crazy about your religion, you do not love me as you once did." A father or mother may say to their own son or daughter, "What ever happened to you! Once you loved us and made us happy, but now you seem to despise us. You have gone crazy over Jesus and the Bible and you do not care for us any more!" What has happened is that the love of Jesus Christ in a good Christian's heart is so far above and beyond all other love that it simply seems to make other affections as nothing. The love for others seems to be not much better than hate, compared to the love a good Christian has for Jesus Christ!

Mrs. Jonathan Goforth, wife of the famed Presbyterian

missionary to China, tells how when she became engaged to the poor, ill-dressed Canadian student, the two lovers had the agreement that Jesus Christ should be absolutely first. She agreed gladly. Though raised in a well-to-do and cultured family, she really loved Christ. But she found the covenant striking close to her heart when the young lover asked her to forgo an engagement ring, that the money might be spent for tracts in Chinese, to save souls in the heathen nation which God had laid upon his heart! And again and again Mrs. Goforth testified that Jesus Christ was first with Jonathan Goforth. Christ was first though it meant poverty, and persecution, and terible privation in China. Christ was first when disease in that pestilence-ridden country took his own children. Many a wife might have grieved that the husband had lost his love for her, but Mrs. Goforth knew that no one can be a disciple of Jesus Christ if he does not hate his father, his mother, brothers, sisters, his wife and children, "yea, and his own life also."

Let no reader feel that he can be a good disciple of Jesus Christ unless Jesus Christ takes precedent over every other love, every other loyalty, every other tie, every other pleasure in this world! For "whosoever he be of you that forsaketh not all that he hath, he cannot be my disciple," Jesus said.

JESUS CALLS US

Jesus calls us; o'er the tumult
  Of our life's wild, restless sea,
Day by day His sweet voice soundeth,
  Saying, "Christian, follow Me."

Jesus calls us from the worship
  Of the vain world's golden store,
From each idol that would keep us,
  Saying, "Christian, love Me more."

In our joys and in our sorrows,
  Days of toil, and hours of ease,
Still He calls, in cares and pleasures,
  "Christian, love Me more than these."

Jesus calls us: by Thy mercies,
Saviour, may we hear Thy call,
Give our hearts to Thine obedience,
Serve and love Thee best of all.
—CECIL F. ALEXANDER

4. To Follow Jesus Means to Be Sold Out to Soul Winning

We are prone to forget the obvious. And the obvious truth from the Scriptures is that to follow Jesus means to become a soul winner. He said to Peter and Andrew, "Follow me, and I will make you fishers of men" (Matt. 4:19). It was a very simple proposition Jesus made them; they were to leave off fishing for fish in the Sea of Galilee and follow Him, to win people to Christ and forgiveness and salvation and Heaven. When James and John left their father and the nets to follow Jesus, it was to become soul winners. When Matthew left the receipt of custom to follow Jesus, it meant three and one-half years' training under Jesus, then a lifetime of soul winning, then martyrdom, as the end of a life wholly abandoned to keeping people out of Hell! So it was with all the apostles.

In Luke 14:16–24 Jesus tells the parable of the great supper in which one servant is mentioned, and he was an indefatigable persuader of men to come to the heavenly supper. And following that, to the multitudes who followed Him, Jesus said, "If any man come to me, and hate not his father, and mother, and wife, and children, and brethren, and sisters, yea, and his own life also, he cannot be my disciple. And whosoever doth not bear his cross, and come after me, cannot be my disciple." Then in the same discussion He gave that searching text. "So likewise, whosoever he be of you that forsaketh not all that he hath, he cannot be my disciple." Jesus, when He talked about a disciple, meant a soul winner! No one really follows Jesus, learns of Jesus, becomes like Jesus, and does the work of Jesus, who is not a soul winner.

Again I say, this truth is so obvious that it seems no honest searcher for truth could miss it. One who follows Jesus must be like Jesus, and Jesus Himself was the Prince of all soul winners. It was Jesus who, before the world began, offered Himself to die for sinners. He was "the Lamb slain from the foundation of the world" (Rev. 13:8). When Jesus came into the world, we are told in Hebrews 10:5–9, "Then said he, Lo, I come to do thy will, O God." And that will, this same passage tells us, was to do away with the burnt offerings and animal sacrifices which pictured the Saviour, and instead offer His own body once and for all to pay for sin! Jesus had no other plan in coming into the world. That is why He set His face like a flint toward Jerusalem and the crucifixion. That is why He said, "I have a baptism to be baptized with; and how am I straitened till it be accomplished!" (Luke 12:50). When Jesus was baptized, He was offering Himself to die and picturing His own burial and resurrection. On the Mount of Transfiguration He talked with Moses and Elias "about his decease which he should accomplish at Jerusalem" (Luke 9:31). When He rose from the dead, He urgently laid upon the disciples the plan to take the gospel to every creature and commanded that every new convert should be baptized and taught "to observe all things whatsoever I have commanded you" (Matt. 28:20), that is, that the new converts should be given the same commission as He had given the apostles.

That is the object for which the disciples were to wait in Jerusalem—they were to be endued with power for soul winning. And even now the dear Saviour in Heaven rejoices over one thing more than over all else—over the winning of souls. There in Heaven, "he shall see of the travail of his soul, and shall be satisfied" (Isa. 53:11). The future joy of seeing souls saved was the sustaining thought of Jesus as He hung on the cross (Heb. 12:2). And right now there is more "joy in heaven over one sinner that repenteth, than over ninety and nine just persons, which need no repentance" (Luke 15:7).

Jesus did not come to the earth to make the world better, nor to raise society to a higher level, nor to establish schools and hospitals, nor to elevate womanhood, nor to free slaves, nor to make brotherhood between races. He said, "The Son of man is come to seek and to save that which is lost" (Luke 19:10). And Paul knew the truth of the gospel when He said, "This is a faithful saying, and worthy of all acceptation, that Christ Jesus came into the world to save sinners; of whom I am chief" (I Tim. 1:15).

So, to be like Jesus is to be a soul winner. To follow Jesus is to become a soul winner. He says to every Christian in the world, even as He said to Peter and other disciples, "Follow me, and I will make you fishers of men."

The monk meant well who built a high column of stones and sat there for thirty years pulling up food and water in a basket on a rope, but he was not following Jesus. Those who enter monasteries and cloisters, to spend their time in meditation, or in punishing the body, are not really following Jesus. Those who take vows of poverty and chastity, who dress in sackcloth and gird themselves with ropes, or whip themselves to mortify the flesh, are not really following Jesus. He gave us plain instructions about that—to follow Jesus means to be a soul winner.

Some think they are called to be Bible teachers and that therefore they need not be soul winners. But that is a wholly unscriptural conception. The dear Lord Jesus was the greatest teacher this world ever saw, yet His consuming passion was to save sinners, to keep people out of Hell. Is the disciple better than his Lord?

Paul the apostle would pass for a good Bible teacher in any Bible conference, college or seminary. Yet Paul had the consuming passion to see people saved. He said,

"I say the truth in Christ, I lie not, my conscience also bearing me witness in the Holy Ghost, That I have great heaviness and continual sorrow in my heart. For I could wish that myself were accursed from Christ for my brethren, my kinsmen according to the flesh."—Rom. 9:1–3.

Paul, the man who received the greatest revelation of divine truth ever offered to a sinning mortal, was pre-eminently the soul winner. This was the driving burden that sent him through shipwreck, jails, the gladiatorial combats at Ephesus; through stonings and scourgings; through unspeakable toil; through fastings and watchings; and finally to the block where he was beheaded. Paul, the Bible teacher, was primarily a soul winner. And no Bible teacher is worthy of the name who does not feel the same way.

Some may feel called to deal with youth. But the Saviour, remember, was younger than the average Youth for Christ leader when He was crucified. And the apostles were young men when Jesus called them. But they were to be soul winners.

Some would be children's workers. Well, remember that little children thronged around the Lord Jesus. He took them in His arms and blessed them, and won them, and pronounced a great curse on any who should offend "one of these little ones which believe in me."

Some feel called of God, they say, to alleviate human suffering. They would help the poor, they would visit the sick, they would care for the orphans. Christianity has so moved upon the conscience of mankind that we know we are our brothers' keepers, and that those who cannot help themselves should be helped.

But must one who helps others be content with that alone? I remind you that the dear Lord Jesus went about healing broken hearts and releasing the captives. He healed the sick, He comforted the sad, He restored to the widowed mother's bosom her son who had been dead, at Nain. He had compassion on the multitude. He fed those who were hungry with the loaves and fishes. He opened blind eyes. To the lepers who said, "Lord, if thou wilt, thou canst make us clean," He answered, "I will; be thou clean" (Luke 5:12, 13). Oh, Jesus did have compassion on suffering people, but all that was secondary with Him, and it must be secondary with everybody else who follows Him. To feed a hungry belly may please God, but then if we let the one we have helped go to

Hell, we have not done Christ's will, and we have not followed Him truly. Soul winning had the pre-eminence with Christ, and it must have the pre-eminence with everybody else who is like Jesus, who follows Jesus, who is a true disciple of Jesus.

When Paul raised money for the poor saints at Jerusalem, it was only the means to an end, it was always secondary to the one main thing of getting people converted. No one can follow any Bible pattern as a disciple of Jesus Christ without putting soul-winning first. Those who follow Jesus become soul winners. To you, to me, today Jesus says, "Follow me, and I will make you fishers of men." And again He said it in Mark 1:17, "Come ye after me, and I will make you to become fishers of men."

God may call one man to be a pastor, another to be an evangelist, another to be a teacher; but God calls all of them to follow Jesus, the route of tears, and burden, and toil, and crucifixion—the route of soul winning! No one really follows Jesus except as He is made into a soul winner by the power of God.

Abraham followed Jesus and was a soul winner. Christ Himself was "the Seed" promised to Abraham. And all who put their trust in Christ and follow faithful Abraham in believing in Christ are those to be numbered as the stars of the Heaven for multitude, and as the sands of the seashore, of whom Abraham dreamed, and of whom the Lord gave him precious promises! And when Abraham offered Isaac, he offered a type of Christ and he promised, "My son, God will provide himself a lamb for a burnt-offering" (Gen. 22:8).

Moses, too, must be ranked among the soul winners who knew of Christ and prophesied of Him, and pointed to Him all the way. To Moses, Christ was the rock smitten in the wilderness out of whom flowed the water of life. To Moses, Christ was the manna, the bread that fell from Heaven to feed the multitude. To Moses, Christ was the sin-offering, the passover lamb, the scapegoat that bore away the sins of the people. To Moses, He was the serpent on a pole bearing the sins of the world, to whom people had only to look by faith and be healed of the Serpent's bite and be saved.

Dear reader, do not evade the truth. If you do not give yourself wholly to soul winning, and if soul winning does not become the passion of your life, the constant occupation of your thoughts and efforts, then you are not really a disciple. Unless you become a soul winner, you are not really following Jesus.

II. Bible Examples of Leaving All

In the Bible we find plain commands requiring the sacrifice of everything in order to follow Jesus. And, thank God, in this holy Book we find examples of men who did all that we are asked to do. We find wonderful stories of men who really left all to follow Jesus.

1. Abraham Was an Example of One Who Left All to Follow Christ

Yes, Abraham followed Christ, for Jesus said, "Abraham saw my day and was glad" (John 8:56).

Abraham was required to leave his country, his kindred and his father's house in order to serve the Lord. That is plainly stated in Genesis 12:1:

"Now the Lord had said unto Abram, Get thee out of thy country, and from thy kindred, and from thy father's house, unto a land that I will shew thee."

Note that Abraham had a three-fold command. He was to leave his country, his kindred, and his father's house.

Abraham had many a struggle in trying to carry out this command, in trying to leave all to follow the Lord. That is indicated in the preceding chapter. The last verses in Genesis 11 tell us the following:

"And Terah took Abram his son and Lot the son of Haran his son's son, and Sarai his daughter in law, his son Abram's wife; and they went forth with them from Ur of the Chaldees, to go into the land of Canaan; and they came unto Haran, and dwelt there. And the days of Terah were two hundred and five years: and Terah died in Haran."—Gen. 11:31, 32.

God had already given Abraham his command. So Abraham obeyed part of this command; he left his country. But he did not leave his kindred. He did not leave his father's house. He took his father Terah into his confidence, and the old father took charge of the situation and took Abraham and Lot and Sarai, Abraham's wife, "and they went forth with them from Ur of the Chaldees, to go into the land of Canaan; and they came unto Haran, and dwelt there."

They set out to go to the land of Canaan, as God had commanded Abraham. But I can almost read between the lines and see what happened. Terah was an old man. I imagine he said to Abraham, "Son, why go into that heathen land of Canaan? This land of Haran is a good land. It is not so far away from Ur. Son, I am an old man. You can't leave your father. I am not willing to go so far." And so sadly and disobediently Abraham settled down in Haran. He had left Ur of the Chaldees to go to Canaan. But he did not go to Canaan. He had not kept the rest of the command. He had not left his father's house, nor all of his kindred. He had Lot and Terah with him and he was stranded in Haran instead of being in the Land of Promise!

I know something of the struggle of soul that Abraham went through in those years in Haran. But he did not come to Canaan until Terah, his father, had died. Wasted years! Abraham was seventy-five years old before he got to the Land of Promise.

And still Lot is with Abram, now called Abraham. Abraham had no sons of his own, and every sensible man's heart cries out for a son! And if he cannot have a son, then he wants sons-in-law, or other kindred to carry on his work. So Abraham took Lot, but Lot was a thorn in the flesh. Lot was mad after money. Lot's herdsmen quarrelled with the herdsmen of Abraham. At last Lot departed toward Sodom, and then moved into Sodom. There his wealth increased and his morals decreased. War came and Abraham had to go by night to rescue Lot who had been captured by enemy kings. But Lot was not in the plan of God for the land of Canaan. Abraham should have left him behind. At long last, and sadly, Abraham had to give up Lot. They did not live together. Lot did not in any sense take the place of a son. Abraham's obedience was belated, but he gave up Lot.

But God had promised Abraham a son. So at long last, twenty-five years after he had gone to the Land of Promise, God gave the one-hundred-year-old Abraham a son. Oh, how joyful were Abraham and his ninety-year-old wife! God seemed to have renewed their youth. They laughed for joy over the little one for whom they had prayed, no doubt, three quarters of a century! And so they called the little one Isaac, which means laughter.

But remember that Jesus Christ does not only demand that we give up the worst; He demands that we give up the best! He demands not only that we give up the foul and the ugly and the sinful; He demands also that we give up the sweet and wholesome and the good. The Lord Jesus plainly says that "whosoever he be of you that forsaketh not all that he hath, he cannot be my disciple." One is not only to forsake the harmful, the evil, but also the blessed and the good. One must give up the Isaacs to God as well as the Lots!

So Abraham had to forsake Isaac. One day the sad word came to Abraham. Abraham was told, "Take now thy son, thine only son Isaac, whom thou lovest . . ." He was to take a three-days' journey to Mount Moriah and there in a place God had chosen, Abraham was to offer Isaac upon an altar. His feet and hands were to be tied and a knife was to be plunged into his breast. His blood was to be poured out upon the altar before God. Abraham was commanded to prove that he really loved God with all his heart.

I think Abraham was dazed and stunned by the command. But he had set his hand to the plow and he did not look back. What a long school he had been through! Leaving Ur of the Chaldees; then after long hesitation, leaving the grave of his father in Haran; then having to break with Lot and letting worldly Lot go his way. And now at long last, his dearest one in this world had to be taken from him. God said to Abraham, "Leave Isaac! Forsake him! You cannot be My disciple if you do not give him up!" They prepared for the three-days' journey. I do not know what they told Sarah. I doubt that she knew what God had commanded. So the father and son and servant travelled alone.

I can imagine that the first night the tired lad ate heartily and, with the servant, was soon asleep after the frugal meal was eaten. I can imagine that Abraham lay awake for hours on his goatskin pallet. He heard the cropping of grass by the hobbled donkey. He heard the crickets and now and then the howl of a jackal, perhaps. His heart bled in grief as dark as the black night of Egypt upon his soul. I think he looked up to God with quivering lips and broken heart, for God seemed to say, "Give him up! Give him up! Forsake him! Abraham, you cannot be My disciple unless you forsake all to follow me."

It may be that night that Abraham put a restless hand out from his pallet and felt the soft sand upon which they had laid their beds. Perhaps he lifted up handfuls and let its fine grains flow between his fingers. He remembered that God had promised that his seed should be as the sands of the seashore for multitude. "And now what will I do? How will God keep His promise if He compels me to slay Isaac?" his heart cried out.

But Abraham got up early, with drawn and hollow eyes, and aroused the servant. They broke their fast, perhaps with dried dates or figs, and went their way. Another day passed in the journey. That night (again I imagine) Abraham looked at the countless stars of the Syrian night and remembered the promise of God that his seed should be as the stars of the Heaven for multitude. "How shall this be?" his heart cried. If he were to slay Isaac, what would there be left to live for? Nothing in his life, nothing in his posterity, and very little, he thought, in Heaven. But Abraham went on.

The third day they came to Mount Moriah. God directed them to the very site where would be later the threshingfloor of Araunah the Jebusite, to be purchased by King David, and where Solomon's temple was later to be built. They left the servant and the donkey and Abraham and Isaac went upon the mount for the sacrifice. The lad was accustomed to sacrifices. He knew what it would take. So he said, "My father, . . . behold the fire and the wood: but where is the lamb for a burnt-offering?"

The answer of Abraham was, "My son, God will provide himself a lamb for a burnt-offering."

They came to the designated place. Abraham built an altar. The startled lad found himself soon bound hand and foot. Perhaps he did not struggle. Perhaps he himself was willing to trust his father and trust the command of God. At any rate, Abraham laid hold of the knife that was to plunge into the heart of his son. Abraham gave up Isaac! Abraham forsook him! He was a true disciple.

But God held the hand of Abraham. God let the son live. They found a ram caught in a thicket by his horns, and they offered this lamb as a sacrifice to God.

But as they walked down the mount and perhaps for the three-days' journey, Abraham said, "I have laid him on the altar. I have given him up to God. He is not mine any more." Abraham had given the dearest thing in this world to God and he never took it back. God had accepted what Abraham gave. With Abraham from that time forth Isaac could live or die. He was already given up for God. Isaac was still loved. He was the pride and joy of his aged father. He was the miracle son, given in answer to long prayer. But God came before Isaac and Abraham had, in the language of Jesus, "hated" his son to follow Christ.

2. Moses, Too, Knew What it Was to Forsake All to Follow Jesus

In Hebrews 11:24–27, we are told:

"By faith Moses, when he was come to years, refused to be called the son of Pharaoh's daughter; Choosing rather to suffer affliction with the people of God, than to enjoy the pleasures of sin for a season; Esteeming the reproach of Christ greater riches than the treasures in Egypt: for he had respect unto the recompence of the reward. By faith he forsook Egypt, not fearing the wrath of the king: for he endured, as seeing him who is invisible."

Moses forsook Egypt. He forsook the palace of the Pharaohs where he had grown up. He forsook his foster-mother. He forsook a chance at the throne. He forsook the company of the cultured and rich of his day. He forsook everything held dear by human hearts. He did it to serve God, and he did it by faith.

I think I know something of what Moses went through. I think the foster-mother held on to him and wept. She chided him and said, "Moses, don't you love me any more? I pulled you up in the little basket-boat, out of the edge of the water. I saved your life when they would have killed you as they killed the other Hebrew boy babies. I hired your mother to nurse you. I brought you up in luxury. I gave you every opportunity for learning. I put you, an outcast slave, into the family of royalty. I have loved you with a mother's devotion. Moses, can you leave me now?" I think she pleaded, she cried. I think nearly everybody who knew Moses said he was a fool. At least that would normally be the attitude of people toward one who forsook all that Moses left. But "by faith he forsook Egypt." He did not fear the wrath of the king. He did not hesitate because of the tears of his foster-mother. He did not consider the scorn of even his best friends. He did not count worth while the fact that his own people did not believe in him. God had put in his heart a call and he answered. Moses forsook all. He refused to be called the son of Pharaoh's daughter. He chose to suffer affliction with the people of God, "esteeming the reproach of Christ greater riches than the treasures in Egypt." So really it was the Lord Jesus Christ whom Moses followed. He was a good disciple. And "whosoever he be of you that forsaketh not all that he hath, he cannot be my disciple," Jesus said.

3. Elisha Is Another Old Testament Example of One Who Forsook Everything to Follow Jesus

The story is told in I Kings 19:19–21:

"So he departed thence, and found Elisha the son of Shaphat, who was plowing with twelve yoke of oxen before him, and he with the twelfth: and Elijah passed by him, and cast his mantle upon him. And he left the oxen, and ran after Elijah, and said, Let me, I pray thee, kiss my father and my mother, and then I will follow thee. And he said unto him, Go back again: for what have I done to thee? And he returned back from him, and took a yoke of oxen, and slew them, and boiled their flesh with the instruments of the oxen, and gave unto the people, and they did eat. Then he arose, and went after Elijah, and ministered unto him."

Elijah the man of God knew that before long he would die. Who would take his place? What man with boldness, with faith, with a holy anointing of the Spirit of God, would speak for God to king and people? I think that after prayer he was led to the young man Elisha.

Elisha was evidently a member of a well-to-do family. He was a promising young man. On the big farm twelve yoke of oxen were plowing and Elisha was directing the operation and plowing with one yoke of oxen.

When the prophet of God came by and laid the mantle on his shoulder, Elisha saw that this meant a call from God. He could be a prophet of God! He could be a student under Elijah, an understudy, and in due season he could take the older prophet's place and be prophet in Israel!

A moment he hesitated, then made the grand decision. He would leave it all! He stopped the plow. He first asked Elijah to wait for him. He would kiss his father and mother and say good-by to all the plans of his young life.

He took a yoke of oxen and killed them, and had a feast for the people. Then he arose and went after Elijah. He left the fine plantation to be a servant of the man of God. He left home and oxen and servants to be himself a servant. I do not wonder that God anointed him with a double portion of the Spirit that was on Elijah, and that he, too, became a miracle-working, mighty preacher and prophet of God. Elisha was a good disciple. He forsook all that he had to follow Jesus.

4. The Apostles Left All to Follow Jesus

This matter is mentioned a number of times in the Scriptures.

In Luke 5:11 we are told that James and John and Simon and Andrew "forsook all, and followed him." In Luke 5:28 we find that Matthew, or Levi the publican, at his rich tax-collector's job, heard Jesus say, "Follow me." And then "he left all, rose up, and followed him" (Luke 5:27, 28).

In Matthew 4:18–20 we read:

"And Jesus, walking by the sea of Galilee, saw two brethren, Simon called Peter, and Andrew his brother, casting a net into the sea: for they were fishers. And he saith unto them, Follow me, and I will make you fishers of men. And they straightway left their nets, and followed him."

Here we are told that Simon and Andrew left their nets and followed Him. In the same passage, verses 21 and 22 say:

"And going on from thence, he saw other two brethren, James the son of Zebedee, and John his brother, in a ship with Zebedee their father, mending their nets; and he called them. And they immediately left the ship and their father, and followed him."

These two, James and John, left the ship and their father and followed Jesus.

In Mark 1:20 we are told about James and John, "And straightway he called them: and they left their father Zebedee in the ship with the hired servants, and went after him."

I have called your attention to the several statements in three gospels about the call of Peter, and Andrew, and James, and John, and Matthew. They left all and followed Jesus.

"All" is a mighty big word. It means a great deal.

With Peter and Andrew it meant their nets, that is, their livelihood, their way of life, their support of their families. Can you imagine these men leaving the only business they knew, leaving their only visible means of support they had, and laying it all down for Jesus, to follow Him and learn to be soul winners?

You know Peter was a married man and his mother-in-law lived with him. Jesus healed her in the home one time. I can imagine that that mother-in-law said, "Peter, it's all right to love Jesus and to listen to Him preach. It is all right to give money and to give some time. But you can't leave your family. Your wife and children depend on you. Peter, don't be a fool. You can't shirk your responsibilities just to be a soul winner and to follow Jesus." If she did not feel that way, she was not like any other mother-in-law or any other good friend who did not have strong faith. Peter left his nets. Andrew left the nets. They left the fishing business. Their families may well have faced want and hardship. But they left all to follow Jesus.

In the case of James and John it is even more moving, for they left the ship and their father.

A man's ship is very, very dear to him. Nearly all ships have names and are spoken of as if they had personalities. On the island of Grand Manan, in the Bay of Fundy, I spent two weeks among the fisher folk and saw them repairing their boats. The boat was not only the means of livelihood; it was the dearest thing that a man possessed. The boat was called by a name, was patted affectionately, was repaired and scraped and cleaned and painted again and again. Fishing people love their boats. But James and John left the ship. They, with their father, owned the ship and were with him in business.

And they left their father, left him with servants.

I can imagine that the old man said, "John, you're not leaving me, are you? I can't do without you. We have built up a good business. James, you have been a loyal, good son. You can't leave me now. I'm getting old. I need your help."

I suppose the boys would say to their father, "Father, you have the servants. They'll help you. But Jesus has called us and we must go. We must win souls."

I can imagine that John said, "I looked into His eyes, and I loved Him. I promised to follow Him till I die. I cannot give Him up. I'll go with Him anywhere He says."

I imagine that the father might have said to James, "Son, you always were level-headed—not so dreamy and idealistic as your brother. Surely you have enough practical sense to see that you'll not get anywhere going with Jesus. Sure, He is a good man; maybe He is a prophet. Maybe He is even the Son of God, as He says. But we are practical folks; we have to carry on the business. Don't leave me, Son!" But James, too, had determined to leave everything for Jesus.

I can imagine that the father and mother said, "You don't love your old Dad and Mother. You are not obeying the first commandment with a promise." They did not understand it, but Jesus had plainly said that unless one hated father, mother, brothers, sisters, wives, children, houses, lands—even his own life—one could not be a disciple of Jesus. And they set out to be disciples. They forsook everything!

And so Levi, called Matthew, left his rich job as a tax-collector. I do not know whether he locked the drawers of his desk. I do not know whether he filled out his last government report. I do not know whether he waited until a successor was chosen. I know that he left the receipt of custom and followed Jesus! And praise God, he made a good disciple!

5. The Apostle Paul Also Was a Good Disciple of Jesus Christ

Paul was a Pharisee of the Pharisees, according to the strictest sect. He was circumcised the eighth day. He was brought up in Jerusalem at the feet of Gamaliel, one of the great teachers of the Mosaic law and of the Jewish learning. He was also a Roman citizen born, and that was very important. He had great learning. He was one of the leading Jews of his day. But he laid it all down to follow Jesus. When Paul was converted he set out to leave everything else behind. It is remarkable that the first question Paul ever asked the Lord Jesus, after he knew who He was, was this: "Lord, what wilt thou have me to do?"

Paul was hated by the Pharisees and the Christ-rejecting Jews with whom he had once labored. He wrote to the people of Philippi, where he had been beaten and thrown in jail:

"But what things were gain to me, those I counted loss for Christ. Yea doubtless, and I count all things but loss for the excellency of the knowledge of Christ Jesus my Lord: for whom I have suffered the loss of all things, and count them but dung, that I may win Christ."—Phil. 3:7, 8.

Beatings, poverty, persecution—Paul knew them all. He knew that bonds and imprisonments waited for him. But he said,

"But none of these things move me, neither count I my life dear unto myself, so that I might finish my course with joy,

and the ministry, which I have received of the Lord Jesus, to testify the gospel of the grace of God."—Acts 20:24.

Paul was a good disciple. He bore in his body the marks of the Lord Jesus. He was stoned and left for dead; he fought the wild beasts of Ephesus. He languished in a Roman prison. Finally he was beheaded. But to Paul it was all glory! He was a good disciple of Jesus Christ.

III. Discipleship Means Crucifixion

In the passage we are studying, in Luke, chapter 14, we find that Jesus said, "And whosoever doth not bear his cross, and come after me, cannot be my disciple" (Luke 14:27). In Luke 9:23 Jesus said, "And he said to them all, If any man will come after me, let him deny himself, and take up his cross daily, and follow me." That is really the price of discipleship. It is crucifixion.

So it was for Jesus. The buying of a world in sin meant that Jesus must leave Heaven, that Jesus must offer Himself, take the sinner's place, suffer the torments of the damned, to buy back to God those who would repent and trust God's offered Saviour. Jesus could not evade the cross and do the will of God. So those of us who follow Jesus, who walk in His steps, who would learn of Him and would be like Him, cannot shrink from crucifixion.

To the disciples Jesus asked a moving, and alarming question. He asked, "Can ye . . . be baptized with the baptism that I am baptized with?" (Mark 10:38).

The disciples boldly and with clear faith replied, 'Yea, we are able.'

And Jesus said to them, ". . . And with the baptism that I am baptized withal shall ye be baptized" (Mark 10:39). I do not suppose these disciples understood all that their decision would mean. But they were ready.

So every Christian who really follows Jesus is to lay his life down. That is what baptism means. One follows Christ into the waters of baptism, and in that burial he pictures the death of Christ and enters into the death of Christ ceremonially. That is, he pictures that he himself is a partaker of Christ's death and Christ's resurrection.

All you who have followed Jesus in baptism, openly, publicly proclaiming yourself a believer in Christ and a follower of Him, did you really mean it? Did you mean that you would count this old sinner who was baptized a dead man, and that he was buried away? Did you mean that you were now raised up to live a new life in Christ? Did you "reckon yourselves indeed to be dead to sin"? Well, that is what every Christian professes when he is baptized. We are baptized into Christ's death. We publicly confess ourselves as partaking of His death and of His resurrection.

It is a favorite saying of some that "once Christ wanted people to die for Him, but now He wants people to live for Him." I do not think that there has been any real change in what God requires. He wants everyone to give himself up to die and then whether he lives or dies, it is to be Jesus first, Jesus only. Jesus always! "Whosoever he be of you that forsaketh not all that he hath, he cannot be my disciple," Jesus said.

It means a kind of crucifixion when we say good-by to loved ones.

That is leaving all to follow Jesus. Would you do that today?

It means death to your own will when you follow Jesus. It means death to the things dearest to your heart, whether big or small.

I know an evangelist, a mighty man of God, who never attends a football game. He does not think that football is wrong. He never preaches against it. He loved football so well that he decided to give it up for Jesus. He was halfback on a champion football team in college days and so the game for him enlists a wonderful enthusiasm. But he simply decided that no game was worth that much enthusiasm when there were souls to save and a wonderful Saviour to serve, and so he decided never to attend another football game. It was not a leaving of sin. It was just putting Jesus Christ first and letting no other love be important in his life.

Once in Augusta, Georgia, I spoke to a large group of ministers. The blessed Spirit of God was upon us there, and we solemnly laid ourselves on the altar anew to serve God with all of our hearts. When the meeting was over, a fine Presbyterian minister, vigorous, handsome, intellectual, graduate of Princeton Seminary, told me: "It was golf that I laid on the altar today. I do not mean that I will never play again. I may play occasionally. I simply mean that golf had gotten too important. I have gotten to be good. I sometimes beat the professionals. I love the game. In fact I love it too well for a man who ought to be keeping sinners out of Hell. I left the game of golf today, and laid it on the altar for Jesus."

I hope you will understand what I am saying. I do not believe, and that minister did not believe, that golf is wrong. I think some ministers would honor God better if they took time for recreation and building up of their bodies. But I know that godly young man was right when he searched into his heart and found there that he loved golf too well; that the enthusiasm he had for a game ought to be given to Jesus Christ and His blessed business of snatching sinners out of the fire.

It boils down to this, that that old self of yours must go on the cross, if you are ever to be a real disciple of Jesus Christ. If you don't hate "your own life also," as well as houses and lands, mother, father, brother, sister, wife and children, you cannot be a disciple of Jesus. "Whosoever he be of you that forsaketh not all that he hath, he cannot be my disciple."

Are you ready to die for Jesus? Well, you have to give yourself up to die, in your own heart deny yourself and give yourself up, before you will be fit to either live or die. God may want you to live, but He wants you first to die, to die to self. And then everyday when self climbs down arrogantly from the cross and sets out to rule your life, He wants you to nail self afresh to the cross and then follow Jesus.

IV. One Must Count the Cost of Discipleship

This is such a serious matter that people who would be disciples must solemnly search their hearts, must weigh their motives, must consider the consequences, if they would be good disciples and leave all for Jesus. That is what Jesus said. He said:

"For which of you, intending to build a tower, sitteth not down first, and counteth the cost, whether he have sufficient to finish it? Lest haply, after he hath laid the foundation, and is not able to finish it, all that behold it begin to mock him, Saying, This man began to build, and was not able to finish." —Luke 14:28–30.

One who sets out to be a disciple of Jesus, one who promises to forsake all and follow Jesus, had better first sit down and count the cost. Otherwise his effort will end, not only in failure, but in shame. And Jesus said:

"Or what king, going to make war against another king, sitteth not down first, and consulteth whether he be able with ten thousand to meet him that cometh against him with twenty thousand? Or else, while the other is yet a great way off, he sendeth an ambassage, and desireth conditions of peace."—Luke 14:31, 32.

Here Jesus means that since being a real disciple depends upon a voluntary decision made and repeated and followed up day by day, one ought to seriously consider the decision.

Do you think the Christian life, the life of a disciple, is all joy and peace? If you think so, you should remember that Jesus said:

"Think not that I am come to send peace on earth: I came not to send peace, but a sword. For I am come to set a man at variance against his father, and the daughter against her mother, and the daughter in law against her mother in law. And a man's foes shall be they of his own household."— Matt. 10:34–36.

Jesus is here talking about discipleship, and real discipleship is not easy. It is misunderstanding instead of understanding. It is infamy instead of fame. It is often hate instead of love by those who ought to love you, a loved one.

In World War II, in the midst of those terrible days when England was tried almost beyond endurance, bombed and beaten by the German war machine of Hitler, Winston Churchill called the people of England to be ready for "blood and sweat and tears." It was no easy task to which he challenged them. And shall we expect it to mean less when we come to follow Jesus Christ with all our hearts?

I knew of a Christian wife who prayed faithfully for her unsaved husband. With broken heart she cried to God. At long last the husband was saved. Then he became more and more concerned about soul winning. At last he gave up a profitable business and laid his life on the altar to preach the gospel. Was the wife pleased? No, she was not! She wanted her husband to be saved. She wanted him to quit his drunkenness. She wanted him to quit following after lewd women. She wanted him to bring home his paycheck. But she did not want him to be a preacher. She did not want him to be counted a fanatic and a fool. She did not want poverty for Jesus' sake. You see, many people would be glad to have you be a Christian and be moral and honest, but they will not want you to be an out-and-out Christian, a "fanatical" Christian, a radical Christian. But what the world does not want you to be, Jesus Christ demands that you be. "Whosoever he be of you that forsaketh not all that he hath, he cannot be my disciple."

Then count the cost today. Are you willing to pay the price in suffering, in persecution, in poverty, even in death, if the Lord so wills it? Are you willing to be counted a nut and a fool, a crank, a fanatic, for Jesus? Are you willing to suffer the loss of all things like Paul, to leave home and kindred like Abraham, to leave the nets and the boats like Peter, Andrew, James and John? Are you willing to leave a lucrative job as Matthew the publican did? Weigh the thing well, for you do not want to put your hand to the plow and then turn back.

A rich young ruler wanted to follow Jesus, but he was not willing to give up his wealth to follow the Saviour. In Luke, chapter 9, we learn that one man said to Jesus, "Lord, I will follow thee whithersoever thou goest." But Jesus did not encourage him. "And Jesus said unto him, Foxes have holes, and birds of the air have nests; but the Son of man hath not where to lay his head." We do not learn whether that man followed Jesus. I doubt it.

But Jesus said to another, "Follow me." This man said, "Lord, suffer me first to go and bury my father. But Jesus said unto him, Let the dead bury their dead: go thou and preach the kingdom of God." He wanted to stay with his aged father until the father was gone. Then when the first allegiance had been served, he was willing to give Jesus second place. That would not do! The spiritually dead of this world could bury his father. He was to put Christ first. No other service is worthy of a disciple.

Then we are told, "And another also said, Lord, I will follow thee; but let me first bid them farewell, which are at home at my house. And Jesus said unto him, No man, having put his hand to the plough, and looking back, is fit for the kingdom of God." These cases are discussed in Luke 9:57–62. One should well count the cost.

Yet there are great incentives to be real disciples of Jesus. First, we will be with the Saviour. Oh, when John laid his head on the breast of the Saviour, he was never sorry that he had left his father and the boats and the nets and the fishing. Then you may be sure that that triumphant group of disciples who counted their lives not dear, but laid them down for Jesus' sake and helped to spread the gospel over nearly the whole world in the first century—surely they knew they had made a good decision.

And old Paul the aged, in a dungeon at Rome, wrote triumphantly to Timothy, "For I am now ready to be offered, and the time of my departure is at hand. I have fought a good fight, I have finished my course, I have kept the faith: Henceforth there is laid up for me a crown of righteousness. . . ." (II Tim. 4:6–8a). He well knew that he had made a good choice when he gave up his fellowship with the Jews and gave up his culture, and friends, and standing for Jesus Christ.

Will you leave all and follow Jesus? Will you preach if He says preach? Will you give up your job if Jesus says leave it? Will you say good-by to the dearest friend and loved one in the world? Well, God may not require that you lose them, but He requires that you be willing to lose them, that you dedicate them to God, that you give them up in your heart.

Who reading this will say today, "Lord Jesus, I will forsake all and follow thee"? Then you, too, may be a disciple as well as a Christian.

4

Home, Sweet Home

The Dearest Place on Earth, the Nearest Place to Heaven Is a Happy, Christian Home.

HOME can be almost a hell on earth. The week before this was written in Dallas, Texas, a man came to the home of his estranged wife with a shotgun. She pleaded in vain for her life, then turned and ran. The full charge of shot hit her in the back and she fell, dead. Then the man put the muzzle of the gun to his mouth, blew away the whole side of his face and fell mortally wounded, was carried to the hospital and died without regaining consciousness. That proves, I think, that home can be almost a hell on earth.

In our nation last year there were one third as many divorces as there were marriage licenses. In one out of every three homes in the nation marriage has failed. Dissension, jealousy, suspicion or even hate have turned the marital cup into gall and the air castles of love into ashes. Drinking, unfaithfulness, brutality and desertion played their part in these home tragedies. And only God knows how many homes were miserable besides those dissolved in divorce. Some couples applied for divorces and did not get them; other homes are held together for the sake of children; some wives endure their husbands for financial support, and some husbands keep their wives to avoid scandal. Certain it is that homes are not always happy homes. Homes can be failures, places where families endure but do not enjoy each other. Sometimes family ties are little more than a convenience. Often homes are little hells on earth.

But home was not so intended. The good God who instituted marriage and the family, provided that homes should be a blessing and joy, a refuge of peace and happiness, a haven from trouble and strife and sorrow. God intended that home should be "the dearest place on earth, the nearest place to Heaven."

The First Home, in the Garden of Eden

Little as we think about it, the institution of the home, marriage and family was meant for perfect people in a paradise of beauty! Home was intended to be the last step to perfect happiness in a lovely and sinless world. God made Adam, the first man, perfect and holy, in His own image. And then, even in the Garden of Eden, God said, "It is not good that the man should be alone; I will make him an help meet for him" (Gen. 2:18). So God made a woman and brought her to the man and Adam loved her and she was his wife. Thus God Himself in the Garden of Eden founded the first home. It was the last step needed for perfect happiness on earth in the paradise of God.

After that time the curse of sin entered in and Adam and his wife became sinners and all their descendants are cursed with the taint of sin. Every man and every woman in the world is a poor fallen creature, and nature itself bears the marks of the curse that came with sin. The world has become a place of war, crime, hate, and rebellion against God and unnamable wickedness and violence. Yet when the angels with a flaming sword drove Adam and Eve from the Garden of Eden they brought part of the paradise with them. The loving mercy of God provided that the outcasts from Eden should take with them the Edenic blessing of marriage and love and home! Every home, then, is a part of the Garden of Eden. Every home is meant to be a heaven on earth. Every home should be a refuge from a sin-cursed world all about us and a likeness of our heavenly home which God has prepared for those who love Him.

The Christian Home Depends on a Christian Marriage

Happiness in the home depends on having God there and having the home honor Christ. Only where Christ is Lord can happiness have full place. If we expect to have a little bit of Heaven in our home, then we must have Christ there, and His will must be done. Sin brings trouble and heartache. It always has; it always will. Sin broke up the Garden of Eden. Sin has brought death into the world. Every sickness, every failure, all the trouble, misunderstanding, and heartbreak of the world has been brought in by sin. So the only way to have a really happy, blessed home is to have a Christian home, a home where the principals in the marriage are saved people putting Christ first.

It is dangerous and foolish for a Christian to marry one who is not saved.

Can Christ and Satan both be Lord in the same house? Can you mix Hell in with Heaven and still make the home happy? Can one expect when a Christian marries a child of Satan that their union, the most intimate of all human relationships, will be a happy one? No, no! The marriage of a Christian to an unsaved person is a sin against God, and the certain result is misery and unhappiness.

I have often seen, as you have, the happy case where God has answered the tearful prayers of a wife for her unsaved husband, or of a husband for his unsaved wife. Sometimes after many years prayer has been answered, and the loved one, married years ago in defiance of the plain command of God (a sinful marriage it was), is saved. God's mercy is great. God is willing to forgive sin. Yet every pastor knows, every evangelist knows, that the most frequent and heartbreaking failure of an answer to prayer is that of a wife praying for her husband whom she married in sin, contrary to the command of God. Many times such are never saved, or are saved after much suffering and trouble in the home. A Christian, marrying an unbeliever, sins against God and makes sure of trouble.

In II Corinthians 6:14–18, God's Word says:

"Be ye not unequally yoked together with unbelievers: for what fellowship hath righteousness with unrighteousness? and what communion hath light with darkness? And what concord hath Christ with Belial? or what part hath he that believeth with an infidel? And what agreement hath the temple of God with idols? for ye are the temple of the living God; as God hath said, I will dwell in them, and walk in them; and I will be their God, and they shall be my people. Wherefore come out from among them, and be ye separate, saith the Lord, and touch not the unclean thing; and I will receive you, And will be a Father unto you, and ye shall be my sons and daughters, saith the Lord Almighty."

Righteousness with unrighteousness is mismated. Light mated with darkness is sin. Christ does not have concord with Belial. He that believeth should not have part with an infidel (literally an unbeliever). The temple of God (the Christian's body) is not at agreement with idols. Therefore the command of God is, "Come out from among them, and be ye separate, saith the Lord, and touch not the unclean" (The word *thing* is not in the original. God does not mean an unclean thing, but an unclean person.), "and I will receive you, And will be a Father unto you, and ye shall be my sons and daughters, saith the Lord Almighty."

If home is to be "the dearest place on earth, the nearest place to Heaven," it must be a place where there is basic harmony between husband and wife, harmony about the deepest things, the highest things, the noblest things. In other words, Christ must be ruler in both hearts or there can be no Heaven in the home.

And let me say here that human love, however high and lofty it is, cannot guarantee happiness in the home. Here in America we are wont to think that love is the sum of all that is necessary to make a marriage successful and happy. But it is not true. I have known cases, and you have, too, where drunkenness, nagging, brutality, incompatibility, dissension and disagreement about the holiest things in life came in homes where love was truly present. An unsaved man's love for his wife will not give him a good heart. An unsaved man's love for his wife may not be able to conquer the demon of thirst for drink. An unsaved woman's love for her husband will not always make her willing to give up the habits and thoughts and plans of a lifetime. Human love is not sufficient to guarantee happiness in the home.

Do you suppose that in two cases out of three, of the marriages that took place in America last year, there was no true love? But two-thirds of the marriages are ending with divorce. Two-thirds of these marriages, or more, will go on the rocks. That does not mean that human love was not truly present. Men and women who could not live together in peace often have told me they still loved each other. It simply means that there must be something beyond carnal, human love, if happiness is to reign in the home.

Human love cannot regenerate the human heart. Human love does not make one Christ-like. Sin abides in the heart that has only human love as a motive. And sin brings trouble anytime, anywhere it appears. Happiness, even in Heaven, would be spoiled if sin were admitted to work its havoc. So home can be happy in proportion as Christ is Lord and as both husband and wife put their dependence on God, love Him and trust Him and put Him first in their lives. Therefore it is folly for a Christian to marry one who is unsaved. God plainly commands, "Be ye not unequally yoked together with unbelievers."

In Rhome, Texas, some years ago, I preached on this subject. The next day a little woman came to me and laughingly said, "I know what you preached about last night, even if I was not here, and I do not believe it!"

"I think you surely must be mistaken. If you know what I

preached, you would surely agree with it for it is in the Bible," I said. "Read this Scripture with me."

So I turned to II Corinthians 6:14–18 and she read it over. Her face became grave, and before she read through the passage, tears flooded her eyes. Weeping, she turned to me and said, "I didn't know it was in the Bible! I didn't know it was there! Why didn't some preacher tell me this fifteen years ago?"

I knew what caused her tears and her broken heart. She had married an unsaved man. Her fourteen-year-old son, following in the footsteps of his wicked father, was now breaking her heart. Just a child he was, yet she could not get him to attend services, could not get him interested in the things of God. He preferred to follow his father. She was reaping what she sowed.

So I feel my responsibility to you young people. I beg you, do not, if you are a Christian, marry an unsaved person. To do so, you sin against God. To do so means certain trouble and heartache. No human quality of character can guarantee a happy home. Human love cannot bring happiness. Only the blessing of God can make the home happy. For your mate, then, choose only one who knows the Lord Jesus and is willing to put Him first in heart and life.

Solomon, the man greatly loved of God, and given wisdom as no other human being ever had, sinned in this matter. Nehemiah said, in rebuking Israelites who after the captivity had sinned by marrying into the heathen people, "Did not Solomon king of Israel sin by these things? yet among many nations was there no king like him, who was beloved of his God, and God made him king over all Israel: nevertheless even him did outlandish women cause to sin" (Neh. 13:26). Marriage with unsaved women caused even Solomon, the wisest man who ever lived, to sin. Such ungodly marriages bring the displeasure of God. They forfeit His blessings, many times, upon the home.

If you have committed this sin, then beg God to forgive

you. You cannot undo your marriage, and you ought not. The Scripture plainly commanded in such places that, "If any brother hath a wife that believeth not, and she be pleased to dwell with him, let him not put her away" (I Cor. 7:12). Divorce is not the remedy for this wrong. Two wrongs do not make a right. Any marriage, recognized by men, is now binding in the sight of God. Your sin is of the past. All you can do now is to beg God to forgive you and to undo, as far as possible, the wrong and harm that have been wrought by your sin.

But to you who have not yet committed this sin, I beg you, beware! Any person who marries one of the Devil's children is certain to have trouble with his father-in-law, Satan! No home can be happy until Christ is the Lord of the home, the King in the hearts of both man and woman. Success, and happiness, and peace in any other kind of a home is only relative, only a fraction of what it could be if Christ had His way in the hearts of both husband and wife. Some wife, perhaps, reads this message who has an unhappy home: your husband is unsaved, or less frequently, some husband will read it whose wife is unsaved. May I say to you kindly, you can never expect real spiritual happiness in your home without Christ in the hearts of those who make the home.

If your loved one is unsaved, then today is the day to do your best. If possible, get that husband or wife today to trust in Christ as Saviour. Make your home united around Jesus Christ. That is the only hope for happiness. Or if you who read this are unsaved, you are the fly in the ointment in your home. If you are unsaved in a home where others are Christians, then you are the serpent in the Garden of Eden. "There is no peace, saith my God, to the wicked" (Isa. 57:21). Your home cannot be fully happy without Christ. Turn to Christ today and make your home happy with His presence.

Little Children Needed to Make a Happy Home

In the Garden of Eden God founded the first home. A

happy paradise it was! There, we are told, "God blessed them, and God said unto them, Be fruitful, and multiply, and replenish the earth, and subdue it" (Gen. 1:28). Even if man had not sinned, God planned that the family should have children. And after sin had brought the wreck of the whole world, and God had swept away civilization in the flood, God repeated the same command to Noah in Genesis 9:1: "And God blessed Noah and his sons, and said unto them, Be fruitful, and multiply, and replenish the earth." I know that there are some homes that cannot have children. God does not always give the blessed privilege of motherhood and fatherhood to men and women in marriage. But in Bible times, barrenness was regarded as a calamity. If you hear the pleading prayer of Hannah, the long continued supplication of Sarah, the way Isaac interceded for his wife, Rebekah, the jealous competition between Leah and Rachel, the joy of the aged Zacharias and Elisabeth when the angel promised the birth of John the Baptist, you know that according to Bible standards, children are essential to the fullest happiness in the home. "As arrows are in the hand of a mighty man; so are children of the youth. Happy is the man that hath his quiver full of them" (Psa. 127:4, 5).

Let modern women be more concerned, if they must, about their schoolgirl complexions and their slender, lovely forms. The painting of the nails, rouge on the face, lipstick and permanent waves—these may be the highest themes of thought and ambition of many modern women. But let us be sure that these never did satisfy a heart nor make the home happy. It is said that while children are little they trample upon your toes, and when they are grown, they trample upon your heart. I suppose that is true for most people. Well, then, let us have them trampling on our toes, and if it must be, let us have them trampling upon our hearts, but God deliver us from an old age without children! Women had better learn to fear, as Bible women did, barren lives, fruitless wombs and breasts that never gave suck. God help me that, after all the sorrows and toil and gray hair the children may bring, I may yet rejoice to hold my grandchildren in my arms and see my children grown and happy and prosperous in the blessing of God, serving their fellowman and giving their testimony for Christ! Children cost! Certainly they cost, from the heaviness of the mother and the pangs of childbirth, on down to the burdens of their adulthood. But children, rightly raised, reared in the fear of God, saved by His grace, trained and admonished in His Word—such children are worth all they cost and more!

I know homes that are never happy. Wives spend money and time, depending upon form and skin and clothes and hair dressing and jewels, to hold the love of husbands. What they need is little mutual bodies they can love and handle and train; little minds that they can enlighten together. Homes would not be so easily broken if they had a real tie of flesh and blood. A man and wife whose blood has mingled in the veins of their offspring will not so quickly separate. Those who have watched beside the same little sickbed, have prayed together and had their prayers answered as they listened so carefully to the doctor's verdict—surely they have something that will hold them together as they override many storms of a nagging tongue, neglect or abuse. I advise every husband and wife who can do so to have children, particularly if they are Christians and fit to rear children.

May I say that part of the grief, sin, violence, and wickedness that is coming upon this old world at the present time is to be blamed on the so-called Christian homes. The homes of the poor, the unlettered, the shiftless, continue to multiply. In the homes of college graduates, well-bred, well-trained, cultivated people, children are scarce. If the men and women best fitted to be fathers and mothers have large families of children reared in the nurture and admonition of the Lord, our civilization would have salt enough to keep it from destruction that is threatening it today. Only eternity can tell how preachers' children have blessed the world. Why should the man who develops only his muscles have more children than the man who develops his mind and character? Some homes can be happy if, in the will of God, He sees fit to withhold the blessings of children. But all who can have children, we believe, should do so, and that home reaches its highest and fullest joy only God intended when there are father and mother and children together, to please God and give their best to Him.

Discipline and Authority in the Home

There can be no happiness without authority. The kingdom of Christ can never come on earth until His will is done here as it is in Heaven. Only when rebellion came in was man cast outside the garden, a fallen soul. No home can be happy without authority.

Here is the basis of all sin: rebellion against authority. The reason for all the crimes against society is this one thing—rebellion against authority. We spoke at a county jail the Sunday afternoon before this was written. Four hundred sixty-five men and women were there. Every one of them, however diverse were their crimes, came there because they rebelled against authority. Every man in the penitentiary goes there for that very reason. Every person in Hell goes there primarily because he rebels against the authority of God and refuses to obey His commands, refuses to trust God's Son, refuses to surrender to His will. We must remember that "the powers that be are ordained of God" (Rom. 13:1). God demands obedience to law, obedience to authority. In the home that must be true if you are to have the blessing of God and peace, if home is to be a little bit of Heaven upon earth. Rebellion means crime and sin, and these always bring unhappiness. For this reason God has provided that the wife should be subject to her husband. He said to Eve, just outside the Garden of Eden, "Thy desire shall be to thy husband, and he shall rule over thee." And so in the New Testament even, women are commanded to be in subjection and under obedience to their own husbands (Eph. 5:22, 23; I Pet. 3:1, 6; Titus 2:5).

How necessary, then, that the children God gives a home should be under authority! God commended Abraham, and confided His plans to Abraham as He explained; "For I know him, that he will command his children and his household after him, and they shall keep the way of the Lord, to do justice and judgment; that the Lord may bring upon Abraham that which he hath spoken of him" (Gen. 18:19). Eli, in the days of the baby Samuel, was a devout and godly man. Yet upon him and his whole posterity there came the curse of God, "because his sons made themselves vile, and he restrained them not" (I Sam. 3:13). God said that Eli, in not controlling his children, "honourest thy sons above me" (I Sam. 2:29).

This duty of discipline in the home is one of the cardinal doctrines in the Bible. So strict was God's plan about it that a father and mother were commanded to see their son stoned if he were rebellious and would not hearken unto them (Deut. 21:18–21). Rebellion in the home is counted as one of the sins worthy of death, along with murder, rape, and kidnapping!

You recall that "honour thy father and thy mother" is one of the Ten Commandments, which compose all the law of God. Fathers and mothers were commanded to "chasten" the son, and if he were still rebellious and would not heed and became a drunkard and a glutton, a rebel, he was, under Mosaic law, to be counted an enemy of society and executed.

So important is this matter of the discipline of children that in the New Testament it is plainly forbidden that a man should be bishop or pastor of a church, if he has children accused of riot or unruly (I Tim. 3:1–5). Again, it is required of one who is to be a pastor that he be one "having his children in subjection with all gravity; (For if a man know not how to rule his own house, how shall he take care of the church of God?)" (I Tim. 3:4, 5).

Do you believe in whipping children? The Bible is as clear on that as it could possibly be. Turn with me to Proverbs 13:24: "He that spareth his rod hateth his son: but he that loveth him chasteneth him betimes."

True parental love must demand discipline. The parent who does not love his child enough to punish him for sin, encourages a career of wickedness that must bring unhappiness and perhaps ruin. Do not spare the rod, you who love your children. Chastisement goes with love, according to the Word of God. Again we have the plain command in Proverbs 19:18: "Chasten thy son while there is hope, and let not thy soul spare for his crying."

I have known some parents who never cross their children except just enough to make them angry. My father had a way of whipping until we cried and then whipping until we quit crying! Brother, if you expect to be honored in your old age, and your children to rise up and call you blessed, then "chasten thy son while there is hope." One day, when he is out from under your thumb and will not listen to you, it may be too late, but while there is hope, chasten him! To hear some modern educators talk, one would suppose that to leave stripes upon the body of a child were a terrible offense. But the Word of God says, "The blueness of a wound cleanseth away evil: so do stripes the inward parts of the belly" (Prov. 20:30). Stripes on the back, in time, save many a wound in the heart later for the child whom you love.

Many people believe that everything depends upon chance; that no one can know definitely how their children will turn out. Sometimes people say to the preacher, "You may talk now, but you never know how it will be with your own children." Well, at least I know that God has promised this, "Train up a child in the way he should go: and when he is old, he will not depart from it" (Prov. 22:6).

As a pastor of a country church years ago, I preached on the subject of a Christian home. One man, a member of the church, came to me with a good deal of indignation and said,

"Pastor, you must go home with me." At his insistence I finally excused myself from others with whom I had agreed to visit, and went to his home. There he said to me, "Pastor, I do not believe what you preached this morning. It simply isn't so!"

I answered back, "What is there I preached that isn't so?"

"It is simply not true that if you train a boy right he will not leave the right way after he is grown. I know I did raise my boy right!"

After a good deal of inquiry, he finally sadly admitted to me that his boy was in the Texas Penitentiary at Huntsville. I said to him, "Now that you have made an issue of it and have denied the statement of God's Word on this question, answer me this: Did you raise your boy right?"

He insisted that he did, but I pressed the matter, "Did you ever have family worship in your home?"

"No," he said. They had been busy people, working on the farm and never had time for such things like some city people did.

"Did you try to win your boy to Christ when he was small and you had influence over him?" I asked.

"No," he said, "I never did believe in begging little children into the church and overpersuading them."

I showed him what the Bible taught about it. "Suffer the little children to come unto me, and forbid them not: for of such is the kingdom of God" (Mark 10:14). I showed him the command in the Bible, "And thou shalt teach them diligently unto thy children, and shalt talk of them when thou sittest in thine house, and when thou walkest by the way, and when thou liest down, and when thou risest up" (Deut. 6:7).

Then I asked him, "Did you whip your boy and make him obey when he was at home?"

He answered, "See here, Preacher; you cannot treat all children alike. My boy was a nervous, high-strung boy, and he couldn't be punished like others could. It would just make him worse instead of better."

And then I honestly and faithfully told this father that he himself had sinned and that his boy was in the penitentiary because he had not followed the plain commands of God's Word about chastening his son and training him in the way he should go.

Is Whipping Children Cruel?

Does it seem a cruel thing to whip a child? If you think so, then listen again to the Word of God:

"Withhold not correction from the child: for if thou beatest him with the rod, he shall not die. Thou shalt beat him with the rod, and shalt deliver his soul from hell" (Prov. 23:13, 14).

The doctor is not cruel who operates upon a sufferer to save his life. There may be some pain in the operation but the end to be attained is worth it all. The parent is not cruel who insists on long hours of study for the child in getting an education. The burden may be heavy, but the end attained is worth it. So the parent is not cruel who whips his child, severely if need be, frequently if necessary, persistently and reverently and prayerfully but determinedly, until he gets obedience and that meek and quiet spirit of reverence and obedience to authority. Whip your children, readers, when they need it. They will not die; rather in old age they will rise up to call you blessed. "Thou shalt beat him with the rod, and shalt deliver his soul from hell."

Doubtless many are in Hell now because their parents never taught them sin must be punished. They never did learn that "the wages of sin is death" (Rom. 6:23). They never did learn, "Be sure your sin will find you out" (Num. 32:23). They never did learn from their parents, "Be not deceived; God is not mocked: for whatsoever a man soweth, that shall he also reap" (Gal. 6:7). They never did learn that turning to one's own way brings heartache, suffering, trouble, condemnation. Many, I say, are doubtless in Hell because they were not punished for sin as children. Parents, as you love God and believe His Word, as you love your children and long for them to grow into good men and women, with the favor and blessing of God, then *demand obedience,* demand careful, quiet, immediate answers to questions, demand obedient action when you speak. Yes, teach your child that rebellion is as the sin of witchcraft and idolatry (I Sam. 15:23). By so teaching him now, you may have tears and heartache. You may be misunderstood. You may often despair and think you are failing. But one day, thank God, you will see the reward and will find that it pays to do what God has said. There is no way to have a happy home without discipline.

Do you know why many a mother is brought to shame by her children? Proverbs 29:15 tells us, "The rod and reproof give wisdom: but a child left to himself bringeth his mother to shame." Again Proverbs 29:17 says, "Correct thy son, and he shall give thee rest; yea, he shall give delight unto thy soul." Oh, the joy of well brought-up young people, quiet, reverent, obedient, respectful! Such children are easy to win to Christ. They find it easy to hold a job when they get one. They learn to study, learn to work, learn to avoid sin. God gives you some twenty years to make men and women out of your children. Be careful that you do not sin by avoiding punishment. Chastening is in God's plan of raising children! The home that does not have strict discipline is not a Bible kind of home. It will not have the peace of God long upon it.

The Boy Who Killed His Mother Was Never Spanked

A few years ago the following appeared in the daily papers:

"DAD FORGIVES BOY WHO SLEW HIS MOTHER"

"CHICAGO, ILL., March 5 (UP).—Theodore Danielsen, who thought he had been bringing up a musical

genius, decided today to forgive his son for killing his mother.

"Danielsen interviewed his 16-year-old son, Theodore, Jr., in jail last night. Teddy told him that he had killed his mother with a bread knife. Father and son wept together and the father listened to the boy's story, his arms around him, his head bowed.

" 'I'm still your friend,' the father said. 'Keep your chin up. You're all I have left.'

"To police, Danielsen said:

" 'He has a very quick temper. We never spanked him.'

"Teddy played the piano well and his teachers called him an 'embryonic genius.' Mrs. Danielsen, who also played the piano well, made him practice daily.

"Teddy killed her Thursday. She was making a cherry pie in the kitchen. He came in. She had learned that he hadn't been to school for two weeks. She reprimanded him and he picked up the bread knife off the table and ran it into her throat. He took $5.00 and jewelry from his mother's purse and fled. Police arrested him yesterday.

"Teddy told the police that he killed his mother because she slapped him and scratched his cheek and seemed about to slap him again."

"HE HAS A VERY QUICK TEMPER. WE NEVER SPANKED HIM!" That is the reason he had such a temper! *The Dallas Journal* commented editorially about this case, that here is youth left free to express itself, without restraint. Dear friend, happiness does not come to the home that has no authority, no discipline, no restraint, no punishment of sin. If you want the peace of God to abide in your home, then, Husband, Father, take your place as the minister of God, the head of the home, and see that righteousness prevails there. It will take prayer, tears, pleading, and sometimes chastising. It will take good example and earnest seeking after the right. But it is worth it, and there is no other way to have a home where God can abide in great blessing.

The Bible is never out of date, and in this matter it is as infallibly correct as it is on the plan of salvation. The home which is "the dearest place on earth, the nearest place to Heaven," is a home where there is peace and order, with a reverence and respect for authority, which, in the last analysis, means a respect for God and a surrender to His will.

Christ Must be Put First in the Home

Homes that are like Heaven must put Christ first. He was first in the creation. He it was who met Adam and talked with him in the Garden of Eden. God has planned that in Him all things should consist and that in all things He should have the pre-eminence. God has committed all judgment to the Son. Jesus Himself said, "All power is given unto me in heaven and in earth" (Matt. 28:18). So, then, if you would have a happy and blessed home, put Christ first.

What part does the church have in your home? Is it counted an honor to be a church member? When you move your residence, do you immediately put your membership in a church of God's leading and choice, in the new community where you reside? And do you regularly attend the services whenever the doors are open? Are you in your place in Sunday School, in the morning and evening preaching services on Sunday, in the prayer meeting on Wednesday night? Do you take some active part, to fulfill your ministry, your stewardship of the gospel? If not, how could you expect God to make such a home happy? Children will not follow the precept of a father and mother whose example does not tell the same thing. It is a pitiful thing that it should ever be necessary to say about parents, like Jesus said about the scribes and Pharisees, "Whatsoever they bid you observe, that observe and do; but do not ye after their works: for they say, and do not" (Matt. 23:3). Children will have no confidence in the hypocrite. They know whether you mean business for God. When they see you day by day putting business before the church, putting your pleasure before God, putting money-making before soul winning, reading other literature before reading the Bible, do you suppose they believe in the sincerity of your claims as a Christian? Do you suppose they are impressed by your devotion to God? Do you suppose they see any reason for trusting Christ and loving Him and serving Him? So, about many a parent it could honestly be said, "What you do talks so loud I cannot hear what you say!" Put Christ first in your home if you want the peace of God to dwell there. We have it plainly said in the Word of God, "I the Lord thy God am a jealous God, visiting the iniquity of the fathers upon the children unto the third and fourth generation of them that hate me" (Exod. 20:5). You may expect your children to follow in your footsteps. You cannot expect them to love God and serve Him, to put Him first, unless you do the same.

At our home as a boy (it is one of my happy memories!) we always expected to go to church. My father, my stepmother, the whole family (too many to ride in one carriage!) went to church. We went when it was cold, we went when it was hot. We went when it rained, we went when it was dry. It was rare indeed that any were so sick they could not go, and if that were true, the rest of us went to church, and just one stayed at home to take care of the sick, if necessary. We went to church and Sunday School on time. We went to prayer meeting. I thank God for the happy memories that proved to me the sincerity of my father's faith in God.

Is Christ put first in your home? Do you have thanks at the table? Are little children taught to bow their heads and to be grateful to God for daily bread? Remember the disciples who went down to Emmaus in their sadness and were cheered with the presence of One whom they did not know. They recognized Him by the blessing of the bread! And your children can recognize Christ in you when they are accustomed to daily prayer, gratitude, to reverence in the home. Does your home have Christian mottoes, Scripture verses on the walls? Are the children accustomed to hearing Mother and Father pray? Are they taught to lift their little voices in thanks and in petition? Are they accustomed to the Word of God as the fountain of blessing which Father and Mother have found it to be? I beg you, put Christ in your home if you want happiness there!

Once I was in the home of a good man who had just died. He was a Christian. He said he was ready to go, and his family believed him. But they said to me, "O Brother Rice, but we never heard him pray! If we could only have heard him pray!" Home can only be a little bit of Heaven upon earth as Christ is recognized as the head of the home.

I am certain that even poverty and the attendant evils and sorrows of it are usually caused by our sins. The home where Christ is honored with the first-fruits of all the increase is usually a prosperous and happy home. Every home should expect the blessing of Malachi 3:10, "Bring ye all the tithes into the storehouse, that there may be meat in mine house, and prove me now herewith, saith the Lord of hosts, if I will not open you the windows of heaven, and pour you out a blessing, that there shall not be room enough to receive it." Remember that Jesus Himself promised, "Give, and it shall be given unto you; good measure, pressed down, and shaken together, and running over, shall men give into your bosom" (Luke 6:38). And where want, and poverty, and stark hunger is, it is likely true that those who have sowed sparingly have reaped sparingly. Where plenty is, even a modest plenty, with the blessing of God, it is often true that 'he that sowed bountifully has reaped also bountifully' (II Cor. 9:6). Every home can claim the promise of Jesus, "Seek ye first the kingdom of God, and his righteousness; and all these things shall be added unto you" (Matt. 6:33). Daily food can come, like manna from Heaven, to those who trust Christ, put Him first and claim His promises. Let every home, then, make

God first in money matters and expect God's blessing in money matters.

Win Children to Christ

Blessed is the father who assumes the responsibility for the salvation of his children. Such fathers have come to me many times with great rejoicing to tell me when the last child has been converted, "Brother Rice, the last one is saved! We are all in the family of God and the circle will not be broken!" The home cannot be happy when a prodigal boy or a wayward girl breaks the heart of Mother and Father. The home cannot be happy where the children grow up and forget Mother's God and Father's God. The only sure hope for happiness through the years is that each child, as he comes to the years of accountability, be won to Christ, to love Him, to trust Him, to follow Him in baptism, to get in the church with God's people, to obey the Lord and grow in grace. If you want the happiness in your home, win your children to Christ.

I remember what I wrote fourteen years ago about my new baby. I said, "Just a few months ago God gave us our baby, Sarah Joy. The other five children had all been converted. We had rejoiced more than once that now all of our little ones had found peace in Christ and we would be a united family in Heaven. And now, with the joy that comes with our five-months-old baby, there comes also a heavy responsibility that we cannot shake off. I have just been thinking, What if we should all get to Heaven but this little one, and she be left outside! I have gotten accustomed now, with some difficulty, to speaking of 'my six little girls' where I used to speak of 'my five girls.' Wouldn't it be a sad and terrible tragedy if, when we get to Heaven, Mrs. Rice and I would have to speak again of 'our five little girls' and never mention the other, because we failed to win her to Christ? I thank God that He helped us with the other five, and that they each one, when they were five or six years old, were taught to trust in Christ, and did. With prayer, with tears, with deep anxiety, the other children were won to Christ. I will never forget how happy we were when the first one, Grace, found the Saviour. What a load lifted! Then with Mary Lloys, the second girl, in 1930 while her mother was reading to her the story of the crucifixion from Matthew, suddenly burst into tears and said, 'Mother! Mother, I want to be saved!' And when little Joanna, the last one, found Christ, not long ago, we were so happy. Now, what if the last one should grow up without any faith in her father's God, without loving Christ or trusting Him? What if she should wander away in sin and break our hearts? Home could not be happy as it ought to be with one prodigal. So, father and mother, I beg you, win your children to Christ." Thank God, that baby girl, now fourteen, has long been a devoted Christian. How glad I am that we have a united Christian family for earth and Heaven!

Not long ago I was reading an old Bible given me by my father. I remember that he had given me to God to be a preacher when I was a baby. I never knew about it until long afterward, after my mother was dead. I learned that she had called me, repeatedly, in letters to her loved ones, "My preacher boy." She had wanted me to preach the gospel and begged God to make me a preacher. Then when I read in my father's Bible, I found underlined the words of Zacharias on the birth of his dear son, "His name is John," and I thought, and my eyes filled with tears, that God had put it in the heart of my father that I might in some sense be a John the Baptist, a preacher in the spirit and power of Elijah, filled with the Holy Ghost, if not from my mother's womb, then at least throughout my ministry! And I wept and prayed that my father's prayers might be fulfilled and that in truth I might live up to my name! Give your children to Christ.

Will I ever forget the day that my mother went home to Heaven? I was only five, hardly six years old. We were called in from our play. In the room, gathered around my mother's bed, were my father and a number of kinspeople. All were weeping except my mother. She said to my cousin, "Georgia, won't you play and sing for me?" Cousin Georgia answered, "What shall I sing, Aunt Sadie?" My mother called for that old song which had blessed her heart so many times,

How firm a foundation, ye saints of the Lord,
Is laid for your faith in His excellent Word!

So Cousin Georgia played it, and tried to sing it, though she could not sing much for weeping. Then my mother called us one by one and had us promise to meet her in Heaven. When we had promised, she looked up and said, "I can see Jesus and my baby now!" Then she smiled around at us and closed her eyes and went to sleep. Oh, the joy in our home because of the mother we had to win us to Christ! I was not saved then, but a little later I was converted, and the joy and peace of certainty of my heart on the matter of Christ and the Bible, is largely guaranteed by the testimony of my sweet mother who is in Heaven!

"Christ Is the Head of this House"

In southwest Texas some years ago I went into a home hoping to win someone to Christ. There I found a newborn baby, three days old. The mother's heart was touched—it was her firstborn. I asked her if she wanted me to pray for him, and she gladly assented. I stooped over to put my hands upon the little red-faced fellow and to ask God to bless him, then I thought, But what about the mother? So I asked her if I might pray for her, too. I said to her, "You will need the blessing of God to raise the little one. You will need power to lead him right. You need Christ. Are you not a Christian?" She answered that she was not, and she, with some tears, asked me to pray for her, too.

I turned to the proud father who sat nearby. "Are you a

Christian?" I asked. He answered, "No." I looked above the door, and there was a motto,

> Christ is the head of this house,
> The unseen guest at every meal,
> The silent listener to every conversation.

Then I asked him, "What is the meaning of this? That motto is not true. That is a lie on the walls of your home. You do not love Christ, you have not trusted Him. He is not the head of this home. Is that not so?"

The father dropped his head. He said, "Well, I know you are right. I guess I will have to take it down. No, Brother Rice, Christ is not the head of this house. I will take it down."

"I know something better than that," I said. "Why not just make it true today? Why not let Christ come in and be the head of this house? Let me pray for you while I pray for your baby, pray that Christ will save you and make you a Christian!"

The Holy Spirit had brought conviction to his heart. He gave his consent, and with a deep concern all of us bowed our heads to pray. I placed my hands on the head of the little baby and prayed that God would help the mother and father to raise the baby for Him, help them win the baby to Christ when he should reach the years of accountability. I prayed that their example would always lead him and bless him. I prayed then that the mother upon the bed, with the baby on her arm, should be saved, that she would fully trust Christ. I prayed that the father would give his whole heart to Christ, claim Him as Lord and Saviour. And they did trust Him, too. When the prayer was over, they took my hand and then and there dedicated their home to Christ. Christ came in to be the head of the house! I know it was a happy home.

Do you want a happy home like theirs? Then let Jesus Christ come in today to be the head of your house.

I thank God for a happy home. I thank Him for a wife who loves me and for children who are sweet and good. I thank God that all have trusted Christ as Saviour. I can truly say,

> 'Mid pleasures and palaces though we may roam,
> Be it ever so humble, there's no place like home.
> A charm from the skies seems to hallow us there,
> Which, seek through the world, is ne'er met with elsewhere.
>
> An exile from home, splendor dazzles in vain;
> Oh! give me my lowly thatched cottage again;
> The birds singing gaily, that came at my call,
> Give me them, and that peace of mind dearer than all.
>
> Home, home, sweet, sweet home.
> There's no place like home,
> O, there's no place like home.

And many another like John Howard Payne, the writer, who never had a home of his own, could write these words, longing for the paradise and peace hereafter which here they have been denied. If you have a home, guard it safely. Let Christ be there and have His way. But make sure of a home in Heaven.

One day we will gather in the heavenly home. Will the circle be unbroken? Are you ready to meet your mother, and your father, and all the loved ones gone on before? If not, then I beg you, get ready. Homes down here are frail things at best. We are troubled with all the sins and failures and mistakes to which the flesh is heir. The best home has been marred by sin. Even where every member of the family is a Christian, sin comes to bring misunderstandings and trouble. When death breaks the ties of home, we say good-by to Mother or Father at the grave. Distance ofttimes separates the chiefest loved ones. Children grow away from parents and leave. One gray-headed companion is left to mourn alone when the other is carried to the Silent City of the Dead. An earthly home at best is but a picture of a heavenly home when God Himself shall wipe away all tears from our eyes. One day Eden will be restored! One day we can meet our loved ones in the paradise of God! Don't you want to meet Him in peace? Don't you want to be a part of the happy home there which God prepares for them who love Him?

> Oh, think of the home over there
>   By the side of the river of life
> Of the saints all immortal and fair
>   In their home in the palace of light.

Today is a fleeting day. In the Father's house of many mansions we can have a home that will never be broken by death or sorrow. Whatever your lot here, with its disappointments and failures, make sure that you have part in the home over there.

Jesus Christ is the way. Put your trust in Him today and have the peace and forgiveness and a bit of Heaven in your heart! Then when He comes for His own we will enter into the eternal rest and joy of Home, Sweet Home, with God!

5

What the Bible Is to the Christian

"And he humbled thee, and suffered thee to hunger, and fed thee with manna, which thou knewest not, neither did thy fathers know; that he might make thee know that man doth not live by bread only, but by every word that proceedeth out of the mouth of the Lord doth man live."
—Deut. 8:3.

"But he answered and said, It is written, Man shall not live by bread alone, but by every word that proceedeth out of the mouth of God."—Matt. 4:4.

"And Jesus answered him, saying, It is written, That man shall not live by bread alone, but by every word of God."
—Luke 4:4.

IN THE Scriptures given above we find it said three times that man shall not live by bread alone but by every word that proceeds from the mouth of God, or by every word of God. In Deuteronomy 8:3 we are told that God humbled the nation Israel in the wilderness and caused the people to hunger and fed them on manna from Heaven, that they might come to know this great truth, that not by bread, but by the Word of God, by everything in the Word of God, a man is to live.

In Matthew 4:4 and Luke 4:4 we find that Jesus, being tempted of the Devil, hungering after a forty-day fast, answers Satan with this Old Testament Scripture. When Satan suggested that He make bread out of stones, Jesus answered,

"Man shall not live by bread alone, but by every word that proceedeth out of the mouth of God."

I would like to help every reader to see what the Bible will do for a Christian. And the texts above indicate that salvation, Christian joy, power, peace, knowledge and success are all dependent upon the Word of God.

It is most suggestive that even Jesus selected this Scripture in the hour of His great temptation and used it to defeat Satan. Jesus was taking His place as "the Son of man." He loved to be called by that title. He represented all mankind. He is the second Adam. He is the example. He is not only the Saviour of all who are God's children, but He is their example, their elder Brother. And here Jesus sets the example for us. We must meet temptation with the Word of God. We must believe the Word, live by it, trust it.

Here, too, is a startling example of what the Bible claims for itself. Of the Scriptures, Jesus said that "every word . . . proceedeth out of the mouth of God." God Himself gave every word of the original manuscripts of the Bible. The Bible, then, is not only supernatural, but it is completely so. It is the perfect Word of God. Every word of it, as originally given, and now as faithfully translated and handed down to us, proceeded from God. Here is the measure of the inspiration of the Bible and so the measure of the authority of the Bible. As the psalmist said, "The law of the Lord is perfect . . ." (Psa. 19:7). Again, "Every word of God is pure" (Prov. 30:5). It is stated clearly in the Bible that ". . . the grass withereth, and the flower thereof falleth away: But the word of the Lord endureth for ever . . ." (I Pet. 1:24, 25; Isa. 40:8). God says, "Heaven and earth shall pass away: but my words shall not pass away" (Mark 13:31; Luke 21:33). The Lord Jesus declared positively that 'not one jot nor tittle shall be done away, until all shall be fulfilled' (Matt. 5:18).

The Bible claims to be the perfect Word of God. Our Lord Jesus believed that claim, relied upon it and lived by every word of divine revelation!

How much of the Bible is reliable? Every word of it! How much of the Bible is profitable and important? Every word of it! For every word of it proceedeth from the mouth of God. The same thought Paul wrote, by divine inspiration, to Timothy, "All scripture is given by inspiration of God, and is profitable for doctrine, for reproof, for correction, for instruction in righteousness: That the man of God may be perfect, throughly furnished unto all good works" (II Tim. 3:16, 17). Every Christian, then, should, by God's help, know all the Bible, love all the Bible, believe all the Bible, follow all the Bible as best he can.

Can anyone say that the dear Lord Jesus did not do perfectly and exactly what we are here commanded to do? The Word of God was His delight, and to obey it was His holy passion! In fact, the Saviour Himself is called in the Gospel of John the Logos, or the Main Thought, or Revelation, or Word of God. Jesus is Himself the Word of God. "And his name is called The Word of God" (Rev. 19:13). St. Jerome was the Catholic father who translated the Bible into *The Latin Vulgate,* the official mother-translation of the Catholic church. Pope Benedict XV says, "So convinced indeed was Jerome that familiarity with the Bible was the royal road to the knowledge and love of Christ that he did not hesitate to say: 'Ignorance of the Bible means ignorance of Christ' ('Prol. in Comment. in Isa.'; cf. 'Tract. de Ps. 77')." And, Pope Benedict XV exhorts all to read and follow the Bible so earnestly and lovingly that "they may arrive at the all-surpassing knowledge of Jesus Christ." (The quotation is given in the foreword to the New Confraternity Translation of the New Testament.) Christ has so identified Himself with the Word of God, the supernatural revelation which is our Bible, that no Christian can claim to be a good Christian who does not with holy zeal set out to know, delight in, and live by the Word of God!

What riches, joy, and blessing there are for the Christian in the Word of God! Dr. Amos R. Wells says:

When I am tired, the Bible is my bed;
  Or in the dark, the Bible is my light;
When I am hungry, it is vital bread;
  Or fearful, it is armour for the fight;
When I am sick, 'tis healing medicine;
Or lonely, thronging friends I find therein.

If I would work, the Bible is my tool;
  Or play, it is a harp of happy sound.
If I am ignorant, it is my school;
  If I am sinking, it is solid ground.
If I am cold, the Bible is my fire;
And wings, if boldly I aspire.

Should I be lost, the Bible is my guide;
  Or naked, it is raiment, rich and warm.
Am I imprisoned, it is ranges wide;
  Or tempest-tossed, a shelter from the storm.
Would I adventure, 'tis a gallant sea;
Or would I rest, it is a flowery lea.

In another message I shall earnestly try to show you what the Christian should do with his Bible. But in this message I long to help you know what the Bible will do for you, what the Bible really is to the child of God.

I. The Word of God Has a Miraculous Part in the Individual's Regeneration

I trust that you, dear reader, know of a time and place and a transaction by which you turned from sin in your heart and depended on Jesus Christ to forgive your sins and save your soul. I trust that you have sweet assurance that your sins are forgiven, that for Jesus' dear sake you are counted righteous on the merits of the atoning blood of Jesus Christ. I trust that God made you His own child by supernatural new birth when you simply received Christ by faith and trusted Him to become your own Saviour.

But did you know that every person ever born of God, every person ever regenerated by the Holy Spirit, was saved partly through the supernatural work of the Scripture?

Speaking to Christians, God's Word given through Peter says, "Being born again, not of corruptible seed, but of incorruptible, by the word of God, which liveth and abideth for ever" (I Pet. 1:23).

Those who are born of God are born of incorruptible seed, by the Word of God!

It becomes clear by the Word of God that no one can ever be saved who does not hear the gospel. The Scripture says that "it pleased God by the foolishness of preaching to save them that believe" (I Cor. 1:21). That is, God saves people by proclamation of the gospel, by some human instrument taking the Word of God to lost sinners.

Jesus said to Nicodemus, "Except a man be born of water and of the Spirit, he cannot enter into the kingdom of God" (John 3:5). Notice the phrase "born of water and of the Spirit." We know that the blessed Holy Spirit is the divine agent in regeneration. The Spirit of God convicts sinners, and the Spirit of God works a miracle of the new life. But what does "born of water" mean? I do not think it means the natural birth. It certainly does not mean baptism. No, the water here seems surely to refer to the Word of God.

In Ephesians 5:25 and 26 we are told how "Christ also loved the church, and gave himself for it; That he might sanctify and cleanse it with the washing of water by the word." Christ saves people and cleanses them "with the washing of water by the word." The Word of God and the Holy Spirit work together in the regeneration of every penitent sinner who trusts Christ. Let us remember it well: no one is ever born of God unless he is born of the incorruptible seed, the Word of God!

"Man shall not live by bread alone, but by every word that proceedeth out of the mouth of God," said the Lord Jesus. And now we see that the very beginning of spiritual life, regeneration, is wrought by the Word of God. A sinner cannot even begin to live spiritually except by the miraculous work of the Word of God, empowered by the Holy Spirit.

How we should love the Word of God, which has been the agent of God in our salvation! How we should delight to live by this wonderful Bible, live by every word of it, since it proceeded from the mouth of God and since our spiritual life itself came through the Word of God planted in our hearts!

II. The Bible Is the Solid Basis of the Christian's Assurance of Salvation

A born-again Christian *may* know for certain that his sins are forgiven. In fact, every Christian *ought* to know that he is God's child, having received everlasting life from God. It is sad that many Christians *do not* know that they are saved.

Again and again when I ask people, "Are you saved?" or "Have you been born again?" they answer, "I hope so," or "I am doing my best." They have no real assurance of salvation. Some people even tell me that they do not believe one can definitely know that he is saved.

I came to Christ as a nine-year-old boy. But for three sad years I had no assurance of salvation. In fact, after my father thought I was too young to be saved and discouraged me from being baptized and joining a church, I threw away my hopes and longed and prayed to be saved. I asked God to save me. I asked others to pray for me. And yet I did not feel that I was saved. I cast away all my confidence. I sometimes hoped fleetingly but usually despaired. But one day in a few minutes' time I got assurance of my salvation. I suddenly knew that I was saved. I have not doubted it one time these forty-three years since! How do you suppose I received this sudden glad assurance that my sins were blotted out, that I had everlasting life, that I was God's dear child?

I got that assurance from the Bible. Reading the Bible as a boy of twelve or thirteen I came upon John 3:36 which says, "He that believeth on the Son hath everlasting life: and he that believeth not the Son shall not see life; but the wrath of God abideth on him." There I saw for the first time that it was promised definitely that when I trusted in Christ, depended upon Him, relied upon Him, I received everlasting life. I knew it was so because the Bible said so.

I had often tried to remember how I had felt when I in my heart turned to God and came out openly to confess Christ as my Saviour. I remembered that I had not wept. Another older boy had shed many tears as he came the same day to claim Christ as Saviour. Would I have been saved, I wondered, had I wept as the other boy wept? I did not feel the gladness some Christians said they felt. How much joy must one feel in order to be assured that he is saved? There were many matters in which my heart condemned me; I had failed God in many, many matters. My boyish conscience rebuked me. I felt that I could believe I was saved if I could live without ever sinning or doing wrong. But alas, I well knew that I was still weak and frail and sinful. But now, suddenly, after three miserable, doubting years I found that God's Word clearly stated that when I believed in Christ and depended upon Him, I received everlasting life!

I read on, fascinated. In the same chapter I found that Jesus had promised in John 3:18, "He that believeth on him [the Son] is not condemned." When I had trusted Christ, my condemnation passed away! *The Word of God said so!*

I read on and found John 5:24, which says, "Verily, verily, I say unto you, He that heareth my word, and believeth on him that sent me, hath everlasting life, and shall not come into condemnation; but is passed from death unto life." So when I had heard the Word of God when that godly preacher, A. B. Ingram, in the First Baptist Church of Gainesville, Texas, had preached on "The Prodigal Son," and when I had depended on the Father who sent Jesus into the world to save, there and then, the Scripture says, I had received everlasting life. Thenceforth I could never come into condemnation because I was already passed from death to life! The day when I read and believed those Scripture promises, in a few short minutes I received perfect assurance that my soul was saved. And that assurance came from the Word of God!

And that is exactly what the Bible teaches about Christian assurance. In I John 5:13 the apostle writes by divine inspiration, "These things have I written unto you that believe on the name of the Son of God; that ye may know that ye have eternal life, and that ye may believe on the name of the Son of God." One may know by the things written in the Word that he has eternal life.

In the same passage, verse 10 says, "He that believeth on the Son of God hath the witness in himself: he that believeth not God hath made him a liar; because he believeth not the record that God gave of his Son." For one not to believe the plain promises of the Word of God is to make God a liar. And the same Christian who was born of the incorruptible seed, the Word of God, has in himself the witness, that is, he has the Word of God, wrought in his heart by the Holy Spirit, and he has the Word of God in the Bible. And this divine record, in the Bible, is given in order that a Christian may know that he has eternal life!

If you want to know that you have eternal life, then take some simple promise of the Bible and rely upon it. For example, in John 6:37 Jesus said, "All that the Father giveth me shall come to me; and him that cometh to me I will in no wise cast out." Did you come to Jesus? I do not mean necessarily in walking down an aisle, or in any other public rite or ceremony. But in your heart did you choose to come and will to come, and decide to come to Christ? I am not talking about your tears, nor your feelings, nor your good deeds. Did you come to Jesus Christ in your heart? If you did so come, then He did not cast you out, and He never will! He received you. And the way you can know that He received you and did not cast you out is by believing the plain promise in the Word of God!

Sometimes troubled converts tell me, "I tried to come, I wanted to come, but I do not know whether I came the right way or not." To all such I answer, "If you wanted to come, it was the wanting which God means here. It was the will to come, the choice to come. If your heart came, then you came! And Jesus did not cast you out."

Did you call upon Christ to save you? Then remember that

the Scripture says, "Whosoever shall call upon the name of the Lord shall be saved" (Rom. 10:13). If your heart honestly came seeking salvation and if you asked Jesus Christ to save you, then you should believe His promise that you are saved.

People do not know that they are saved because they feel a certain way. Feelings may come or go. The first time your health breaks down you may lose the buoyant gladness on which you now depend. The first time Satan trips you and you fall into some sin and a burning conscience fills you with grief, you may lose all the assurance which is based on your feeling. You may go through some trial or be so tempted of Satan that you may lose the gladness which you now have. But, thank God, the Word of God abides forever! If your assurance is based on "thus saith the Lord," you need never lose it. The Word of God is the source of true Christian assurance. Do not make God a liar but believe the record that He has given that those who believe on Him have eternal life.

III. The Scriptures Are the Food on Which Christians Grow

Christians often have the idea that attending church services, singing, testifying, along with prayer, are the principal means of Christian growth. We do not deny that a newborn baby should get its exercise. It should be in constant dependence and fellowship with its mother. And so a Christian ought to serve the dear Saviour who has redeemed him, and ought to be in constant touch with God in prayer. Yet the baby does not grow without food and a Christian does not grow without the Word of God. First Peter 2:2 says, "As newborn babes, desire the sincere milk of the word, that ye may grow thereby."

I suggest that you open your Bibles to I Peter and read the last of chapter 1 and the first of chapter 2. First Peter 1:23–25 closes chapter 1, but the chapter division is man's idea, not God's. The Scripture itself was not originally divided into chapters. So the first two verses in chapter 2 go right along with the last three verses of chapter 1. Please look at it in your

Bible. Then you will see that the Scripture here is clearly saying that one is born of the incorruptible seed of the Word of God that lives and abides forever and that therefore one should continue to grow by this same supernatural Word of God. In other words, since the Christian is born of the incorruptible seed of the Word of God, he should live "by every word that proceedeth out of the mouth of God," as Jesus said in Matthew 4:4.

Every new convert, then, should be urged to read the Bible, to read it daily, to love it, to search it, to memorize much of it, to delight in it, to follow it. For Christian growth depends more upon the Word of God than on any other factor. Any Christian who wants to become a mature, strong, robust Christian must settle down to a steady diet of the Word of God.

I have known people who were very active in Christian work who were spiritual babes and spiritual weaklings, starved for lack of the spiritual food whereby Christians grow! I was astonished when a gray-headed woman, active in Christian work many years, told me that she was not sure of her salvation. I have been grieved many times to find active church people mere babies in Christian character, in faith, in spiritual understanding. They were starved Christians. Christian activity, Christian sacrifice, prayer, even devoted soul-winning efforts, do not take the place of feeding upon the Word of God. There is no substitute for the Word of God as food for Christian growth. The Word of God contains the spiritual proteins and vitamins for spiritual muscles and bones and spiritual health and growth. "Man shall not live by bread alone, but by every word that proceedeth out of the mouth of God."

IV. The Scriptures Are God's Way to Daily Victory Over Sin

God wants Christians to live daily victorious lives. And God has provided the means for victory.

Psalm 119:9 says, "Wherewithal shall a young man cleanse his way? by taking heed thereto according to thy word."

Again, in Psalm 119:11 we have the same truth taught: "Thy word have I hid in mine heart, that I might not sin against thee."

Young man, do you want to cleanse your way? Then take heed to it according to the Word of God. Set out to find God's rules for living in victory; you will find them in the Word of God.

Many Christians seek by earnest prayer to have some great experience that they hope will change them so they will not be tempted. They think some "second blessing" will eradicate the carnal nature and that this permanent and continuing victory may be secured by one great crisis experience. However, multiplied thousands have discovered that however great the emotional experience, they still have with them the carnal nature and they often fall under temptation. No, God's way for a Christian to have victory over sin is not through some ecstatic emotional experience, but through feeding upon the Word of God, being washed by it, being taught by it, being warned by it, and being strengthened by it, so that he can meet the temptations. It is well to remember that even the dear Lord Jesus met each of Satan's temptations with a quotation of Scripture. Tempted to make bread and assuage His hunger, Jesus replied, "It is written, Man shall not live by bread alone, but by every word that proceedeth out of the mouth of God." Tempted to cast Himself down from the pinnacle of the temple for a public show, Jesus answered, "It is written again, Thou shalt not tempt the Lord thy God." Tempted to bow down to Satan in order to obtain world dominion, Jesus replied, "It is written, Thou shalt worship the Lord thy God, and him only shalt thou serve." Jesus defeated Satan's worst temptations by the Word. He, the great Son of man, our Saviour and Pattern, will help us to have daily victory also through the Word of God.

To be prepared for temptation, one needs to learn the

Word of God ahead of time and hide it in his heart. It may be too late to load your gun when the bear charges you. It is too late to study your lesson at examination time. So the Christian is exhorted to follow David's example: "Thy word have I hid in mine heart, that I might not sin against thee." Studying the Word of God, learning the truths of the Word of God and memorizing many passages, will give the Christian a strong defense against temptation. By mastering the Word of God, hiding much of it in his heart by memory, and hiding the whole spirit and tenor of its teachings in his heart by reading, by enjoyment, by meditation and by obedience, the Christian will have the will to resist temptation, will have the spiritual strength to overcome temptation and the divine reassurance and help which comes from the living, supernatural Word of God.

How can the drunkard leave his drink? How can the smoker quit his cigarettes? How can the man with licentious thoughts conquer his lust? It is well to pray, but prayer is not enough. It is well to seek the company of Christians; that will help, but it is not enough. He must set out to daily grow in spiritual strength by feeding on the Word of God, by taking it to heart with earnest devotion and hiding much of it in his heart. He may fail, and stumble and fall short, but, praise the Lord, he has the blessed assurance that he will grow stronger and more and more have daily victory over the sins he hates, the sins that grieve God and hurt the Christian and harm his testimony. The Word of God is the Christian's secret of growth and spiritual strength in overcoming sin and in living the victorious life.

Any teaching about the victorious life that does not stress the primary place of the blessed Word of God in Christian victory does not follow fully the Word of God.

V. The Bible, God's Way for Christians to Be Sanctified

When the Bible mentions sanctification for the Christian

it does not mean sinless perfection. That is clear from I John 1:8, which says, "If we say that we have no sin, we deceive ourselves, and the truth is not in us." The Bible does not teach that by one mystic period of ecstasy or by one supernatural crisis the Christian is made sinless and perfect. Good people who think so have misunderstood the Scripture.

But, we must still remember that the Bible has a doctrine of sanctification and holiness. And the Bible, by these terms, means separated to God, set apart for God. So Israel is "a holy nation," so Jerusalem is a holy city, so the Christians at Corinth, though carnal, were "sanctified in Christ Jesus" (I Cor. 1:2). In fact, there is a sense in which every Christian is set apart for God and so is sanctified once for all by the offering of Christ (Heb. 10:10).

But is there a way in which a Christian can more and more be practically set apart for God? How may a Christian man become more and more God's man, separate from the world and different from the world? How can a Christian woman become more and more God's woman, set apart for God's service? How may young people become different from the young people of the world, in outward life and in inward devotion and consecration? The answer is, they may become sanctified by devoted reading and meditating upon and following the Word of God!

In John 17 the dear Lord Jesus prayed for His disciples, not only for the original disciples, but for all that should afterwards believe on Him through their word. Speaking of all of us Christians, Jesus prayed to the Father in these words:

> *"I have given them thy word; and the world hath hated them, because they are not of the world, even as I am not of the world. I pray not that thou shouldest take them out of the world, but that thou shouldest keep them from the evil. They are not of the world, even as I am not of the world. Sanctify them through thy truth: thy word is truth."*—John 17:14–17.

Jesus has given to Christians God's Word. He does not ask that we should be taken out of the world but that God would keep us from the evil in the world. And then He prays that we will be sanctified through God's truth in the Bible. He says, "SANCTIFY THEM THROUGH THY TRUTH: THY WORD IS TRUTH." We are to be sanctified by the Word of God.

In Acts 20 we find that Paul came to Miletus, the seaport town near Ephesus where he had spent three years in winning souls and building the church. He called for the elders of the church at Ephesus to meet him, and there solemnly gave them his charge. Then he said to them, "I commend you to God, and to the word of his grace, which is able to build you up, and to give you an inheritance among all them which are sanctified" (Acts 20:32).

It is true that preachers do a *different work,* a work set apart from the work of the world. But, oh, how we ministers of the gospel need to be *different men!* We need to be men of God, men set apart for God, men sanctified to a holy calling. How may we preachers obtain this blessed result of sanctification? Paul commends us to the Bible which is able to build us up and to give us an inheritance among all them that are sanctified!

I am thinking now of one of the most saintly men I ever knew. I think I must say that he loved the Bible and was moved and affected more by the Bible than almost anybody else I ever knew.

True godliness comes from this kind of sanctification. One who loves the Word, lives in the Word, lets the blessed Word of God have its supernatural work on his heart and life and affections and sins and hopes; on his family, on his business, on his prayers, on his joys, on his friends, on his enemies, on his labors, on his plays—such a man becomes truly godly, or set apart for God. The blessed Word of God is the means of sanctification, the means of true consecration, if we let the Word have its way in our lives.

I am not speaking of a mere mechanical learning of the words nor of a Pharisaic delight in the letter. I am speaking about such holy devotion to the Word as lets the Word have its perfect way with us. If we really "live . . . by every word that proceedeth out of the mouth of God," as Jesus said we are commanded to do, then we cannot but be different! We cannot remain like the world, nor indifferent to God's plan, nor alien from His ways. Born-again Christians still need to learn to be set apart and separated and made holy, sanctified to God and His will and way by feeding on and meditating and delighting in the Word of God daily.

VI. The Bible, God's Means for Growing Faith

The Christian is plainly commanded, "Have faith in God" (Mark 11:22). We are told that "without faith it is impossible to please him" (Heb. 11:6). We are told that if we believe, "all things are possible to him that believeth" (Mark 9:23). Faith is the key that unlocks every treasure house of God and gets everything that God has that a Christian wants and needs. But how may I have the faith which God commands me to have?

It is right that a Christian should pray for faith. The disciples prayed, "Lord, Increase our faith" (Luke 17:5). The father with the devil-possessed boy said, "Lord, I believe; help thou mine unbelief" (Mark 9:24). It is right for us to ask God to increase our faith, but God has His own appointed way of answering that prayer. In Romans 10:17 the Scripture says, "So then faith cometh by hearing, and hearing by the word of God." When this Scripture was written printing had not been invented. Only a few hand-copied manuscripts of Scripture portions were available and very, very few people could read and write. So these Scriptures were read publicly and most people got the blessings from the Scriptures by hearing them. "So then faith cometh by hearing, and hearing by the word of God." You see, the Word of God builds faith.

In a time of trial and testing I delighted to read how the

three Hebrew children who would not bow to the image of Nebuchadnezzar were cast into the fiery furnace and how God delivered them. I delighted to read how Daniel was cast into the den of lions for praying and how God shut the mouths of the lions and Daniel escaped unharmed. I read with the deepest joy and mounting faith the story of Sennacherib's army surrounding Jerusalem and how the letter of his threats and his derision toward God was spread out on the altar by King Hezekiah and Isaiah the prophet and then how the next morning 185,000 of Sennacherib's army lay dead and he returned to his own city and was murdered by his own sons in the house of his idol god! Thank God, I found that the Scriptures gave me courage and faith. I found that God takes care of people who trust Him! I found that one may look through the dark time of tribulation and persecution and know that God will be faithful when everybody else fails.

I remember when I was a young preacher starting, with my wife, to the seminary. I worked a few hours each week with a hoe on the campus at thirty cents an hour. Later I preached in country churches and sometimes got ten or twelve dollars per week, sometimes fifteen. We faithfully tithed during that time and how we did delight to read the words of Jesus who in Matthew 6:25–34 said we were not to take thought for what we should eat or drink or for clothing. Jesus said that the heavenly Father fed the fowls of the air, and that He clothed the lilies of the field, and that all of us who were born-again children should have better care than these! Jesus promised that if we should seek first the kingdom of God and His righteousness all these things needed would be added to us (Matt. 6:33). We believed those promises. Our faith mounted up. And, thank God, now for many years we have lived a triumphant and happy life without fret about our food, clothing, and ordinary needs. We take our needs to God. From the blessed Bible we learned to trust Him! Faith comes by the Word of God!

That is one reason for showing unconverted sinners who want to be saved the promises in the Word of God. Let them see what God has promised. Let them base their decision on the plain Word of God. If they see how clearly He has promised everlasting life to those who put their trust in Jesus, the blessed Word of God will help to grow faith in their unbelieving hearts. Faith comes by the Word of God!

All the mighty men of faith have been mighty men to feed on the Word. Read the life of George Müller of Bristol, the man who prayed down 7½ million dollars from God without ever taking a public collection, without ever writing a friend for money, without making a published appeal or an appeal to a congregation. He supported as high as 2,300 orphan children at once, sent missionaries to many heathen lands, sent gospel literature around the world. And he did it by the prayer of faith. The way he got the faith was by constant reading and meditation in the Word of God. He read the Bible over and over and over, and when he was about ninety years old he declared he had lost interest in all other books but the Bible. And he claimed the blessed promises he found therein. His mighty faith came by a holy absorption in and delight in the Word of God.

Hudson Taylor was a mighty man of faith. He founded the China Inland Mission. He had faith to go himself to China without promised support from anybody. Later he had faith to take hundreds of missionaries for whom there was no definite promise of support from men. But he had learned to trust God. He was a man of mighty faith in a mighty God. But Hudson Taylor was one of the most devoted Bible students this world has seen. He loved the Word, read the Word, meditated in the Word day and night. One of his friends travelling on a riverboat with him told how Hudson Taylor would rise at five o'clock in the morning and light his candle to get a couple of hours with the Word of God before others awoke. His faith came from God through the Bible.

D. L. Moody used to rise at four o'clock or five o'clock in

the morning to study his Bible before others were around. He made the Bible first and so he grew a mighty faith in God. Faith really comes from the Bible. As the Bible becomes your bread and meat, as you begin really to live "by every word that proceedeth out of the mouth of God," your faith will grow mightily.

VII. Living by Every Word of the Bible, the Secret of Answered Prayer

This living by every word that proceeds from the mouth of God, as the Lord Jesus said we should do, is really the basic secret of answered prayer. We have just seen above how the faith that secures the answer grows by use of the Word of God. So every other condition that makes it pleasing to God to answer our prayers and makes it right for God to answer our prayers, is promoted by devotion to and feeding upon the whole Bible. Jesus said, "If ye abide in me, and my words abide in you, ye shall ask what ye will, and it shall be done unto you" (John 15:7). It is good for us to abide in Christ, that is, to be absorbed in Him, to love Him and surrender to Him. But that alone is not enough to guarantee the answers to our prayers. For though we love Christ we may not know what He wants, may not know what He has promised, may not know His instructions. So we need not only to abide in Christ but to have His words live in us. And when we do so abide in Christ and have His words abide in us, then He promised that we may ask anything in the world we want and have it! What a marvelous promise! By having the Word of God live abundantly in our lives is the great key of answered prayer.

One who loves the Word, feeds on the Word, judges his own thoughts and plans and desires by the blessed Word of God, can pray in the will of God, can pray acceptably, and so God can afford to answer his prayers. No one can be sure of praying in the will of God who does not adjust his prayer life to the will of God by the yardstick of the Word.

God feels very keenly this matter of our heart attitude toward the Word of God and He very strictly applies it in this matter of answered prayer. Proverbs 28:9 says, "He that turneth away his ear from hearing the law, even his prayer shall be abomination." One who turns his heart away from the Word has turned his heart away from the will of God. He does not know the will of God, perhaps; certainly he does not *want* the will of God. And that is such a sin and pictures such a sad state of heart that God says such a prayer is an abomination! If you want your prayers answered, then, I beg you, love the blessed Word of God. Meditate in it day and night! Try to live "by every word that proceedeth out of the mouth of God."

VIII. The Bible, the Source of Daily Guidance for a Christian

"Thy word is a lamp unto my feet, and a light unto my path," said the psalmist (Psa. 119:105). The Bible is Heaven's light on earthly pathways. Again, "The entrance of thy words giveth light; it giveth understanding unto the simple" (Psa. 119:130). The Bible is the source of true wisdom, true understanding of the will of God.

Does that mean that a Christian should not rely upon and should not seek the leading of the Holy Spirit? Is it not intended that a Christian should have daily leadership of the Holy Spirit? I assure you, I do not mean to minimize the leadership of the Holy Spirit. Every Christian can have and should have the clear leading of the Holy Spirit on every important step of life's pathway. But we are to remember that the Holy Spirit always leads in conformity to the written Word of God. The Holy Spirit is Himself the divine Author of the Bible. "Holy men of God spake as they were moved by the Holy Ghost" (II Pet. 1:21). The freedom with which the Holy Spirit guides a Christian, His intimate conscious fellowship with a Christian is based on the Christian's attitude toward the Bible. Jesus promised the disciples that the

Comforter would come and abide with them forever, "even the Spirit of truth" (John 14:16, 17). But He explained, "He that hath my commandments, and keepeth them, he it is that loveth me: and he that loveth me shall be loved of my Father, and I will love him, and will manifest myself to him" (John 14:21). Christ and the Father are manifested by the work of the Holy Spirit dwelling in a Christian's body, that is, are manifested *provided* that this Christian has the commandments and keeps them! In other words, in proportion as a Christian loves the Word and follows the Word and meditates in the Word, the Holy Spirit, the Spirit of truth who dwells in every Christian's body, can teach and lead the Christian.

Again, in verse 23 of the same chapter we read, "Jesus answered and said unto him, If a man love me, he will keep my words: and my Father will love him, and we will come unto him, and make our abode with him." The work of the blessed Holy Spirit in guiding and teaching a Christian depends on how well he keeps the words of Jesus Christ, as recorded in the Bible!

Again, in John 14:26 Jesus gave the same teaching. "But the Comforter, which is the Holy Ghost, whom the Father will send in my name, he shall teach you all things, and bring all things to your remembrance, whatsoever I have said unto you." The blessed Comforter, the Holy Ghost, is sent to "teach . . . all things, and bring all things to your remembrance, whatsoever I have said unto you." But how can a Christian have the truth of the Word of God and the words of Christ brought to his remembrance if he never learned them? Any Christian is handicapped in being led by the Spirit if he does not know his Bible. For the Holy Spirit always leads in accordance with the revealed will of God in the Bible.

It is remarkable how often this teaching is made clear in the Bible; that the Holy Spirit guides and leads only as one is willing to take the revealed will of God. For example, in

John 16:13 Jesus said, "Howbeit when he, the Spirit of truth, is come, he will guide you into all truth: for he shall not speak of himself; but whatsoever he shall hear, that shall he speak: and he will shew you things to come."

Yes, the Holy Spirit is to guide in the truth. But the Holy Spirit does not simply guide according to His own independent plan. He takes the revealed will of God in the Bible and helps a Christian to understand that. The Holy Spirit's leading always coincides exactly with the teaching of the Word of God.

A Christian woman told me the other day, "If I were convicted in my heart that the thing you mention is a sin, I would not do it." I called her attention to a plain statement in the Word of God that a certain thing was wrong. She replied, "Yes, I know the Bible says that, but the Holy Spirit does not impress me that it is wrong." In this case she had already closed her mind to the truth and the Holy Spirit would not lead her because she had insulted the Word of God and ignored it. No one can know the will of God by Holy Spirit guidance who is not willing to accept the guidance of the same Holy Spirit already written down in the Bible.

But the Christian who with all his heart searches the Word of God, loves it, meditates in it, and with holy eagerness tries to find the will of God may safely pray that the Holy Spirit will guide him so he can know the will of God in the Bible. And the Holy Spirit, thus ungrieved, will make the Bible live, will give holy wisdom in understanding it, and on any point in which the Scripture does not speak, He will make the will of God clear. But no one has a right to expect the Holy Spirit to guide him on smaller matters where the Bible does not speak, when he does not seek the will of God in the larger matters clearly revealed in the Bible. There is an affinity between the Holy Spirit and the Word of God. They always fit together perfectly. God's Word is the basis of all practical wisdom, the basis of all guidance for God's child.

Should the Christian not follow his conscience? Yes, but his conscience will prove unreliable if he does not constantly train his conscience according to the Word of God.

Does not God intend a Christian to have the counsel of his pastor and other Christian leaders? Yes, but always with the understanding that the Word of God itself is the final authority for every Christian and that all advice of others and preaching of others is to be weighed by the perfect will of God revealed in the Bible.

The Word of God has light on every problem that a Christian will ever face! Learn the Word of God and have the answer to your problems!

As a lad, I wanted to visit with a family where I often went. It was a big family and they had a jolly time. But my father quoted to me the Scripture, "Withdraw thy foot from thy neighbour's house; lest he be weary of thee, and so hate thee" (Prov. 25:17). That bit of divine wisdom helped me then.

My brother and I had some hot words once, and my father quoted the proverb, "A soft answer turneth away wrath . . ." (Prov. 15:1), and I was rebuked and shamed and was taught the better way.

Again one day we needed some farm machinery and I suggested that we borrow from a neighboring rancher. But my father reminded me that the Bible says that "the borrower is servant to the lender" (Prov. 22:7). I did not want to be a servant, and I saw the point at once. There is divine wisdom in the blessed Word of God for every problem a Christian can ever meet. Oh, Christian, take the Word of God as a lamp to your feet and a light to your path!

IX. The Scripture Is Seed for the Soul Winner

Jesus once told a parable of a sower who went forth to sow. This sower represented a soul winner. Then Jesus said, "Now the parable is this: The seed is the word of God" (Luke 8:11). The seed for the soul winner is the Word of God.

Remember that I Peter 1:23 tells us that all Christians have purified their souls in obeying the truth through the Spirit, "being born again, not of corruptible seed, but of incorruptible, by the word of God, which liveth and abideth for ever." Every person who was ever converted, ever born again, was changed by the miraculous work of the Word of God, used by the Spirit of God through some Christian. Every one who is ever saved, then, must be born of the Word of God.

Psalm 126:5, 6 gives us this great rule for soul winning: "They that sow in tears shall reap in joy. He that goeth forth and weepeth, bearing precious seed, shall doubtless come again with rejoicing, bringing his sheaves with him."

Every one who would win souls, then, must carry the Word of God. All the sower's labor is wasted, all his tears are fruitless, unless he sows the precious seed!

When I was nine years old my father moved us to a ranch in West Texas. I was soon put in a field a mile square, driving six big mules to a plow. We broke the ground, then harrowed it, and then sowed the field to grow feed for the wintertime. I remember driving the six big mules to the long grain drill hour after hour. It was a tremendous experience to me to have day after day the responsibility of that big team. I could not harness them alone, but after they were harnessed I could hitch them to the drill, stop when the sun was straight over my head to water them and feed them and eat my lunch under the wagon; then hitch them again to the drill and sow.

After a certain number of rounds on the portion or "land" we were sowing I was always to fill up the big seed box of the grain drill. But once as I drove happily along watching to overlap the wheel track every time all along, and yet dreaming of great things of the future, I entirely forgot to fill up the seed box! Suddenly I remembered. I stopped the team, looked disconsolately in the box which was now empty and wondered how far I had gone with the empty grain drill, actually sowing no seed. I made a wild guess and after filling up the drill, I went back over much of the land. But I did not guess right and when the grain came up there was a strip a mile long and perhaps fifty feet wide which was barren! I was the laughingstock of the countryside. And many a Christian who seeks to win souls will find himself the laughingstock of Heaven if he does not use the supernatural seed of the Word of God in his soul-winning efforts.

It is not the words of men which save, but the words of God. God wants our explanation of the Word, our exhortation, our tears, our personal testimony, our illustrations. "It pleased God by the foolishness of preaching to save them that believe" (I Cor. 1:21). Not only the Word of God, but the *preached* Word of God is used to save people. But God never saves anybody without the use of the Word. This is the incorruptible seed which sprouts in the heart of a hearer and makes him a child of God, by the work of the Holy Spirit.

Let every Christian, then, know that there are two elements that are absolutely essential in soul winning. One is the breath of Heaven, the anointing of the Holy Spirit; the other is the Word of God. If one goes with the heart broken by the Holy Spirit and uses the Word of God, he is certain to come back rejoicing with sheaves.

With what tender earnestness, then, ought the Christian to search the Scriptures! I think a Christian ought to spend hours in memorizing Scriptures and in earnestly searching to understand God's plan of salvation. The gospel ought to become sweet and dear to every Christian, because it is the lifeline he throws to shipwrecked sinners. It is the seed he sows in the ground broken up by the providence of God. It is the light of God in the darkness of sin. It is the bread of God to starving ones. Oh, if you would be a soul winner then learn to love and to use the Word of God! I have known new converts saved in a rescue mission who in a few weeks had more success in soul winning than a preacher with college and seminary degrees. The reason was that the new convert knew and loved and utterly depended upon some sweet verses of Scripture which he used with boldness and with power to get sinners to repent and trust in Christ.

The Scripture is seed for the gospel sower. It is the only incorruptible seed which will germinate and grow to make a saint out of a sinner, to make a child of God out of a child of Hell, to make an unregenerate sinner now regenerated and a partaker of the divine nature. Use the Word of God in soul winning!

X. The Scripture Is the Christian's Constant Source of Joy and Peace

"Great peace have they which love thy law." Psa. 119:165.

If a Christian has salvation by the Word of God and assurance of salvation by the Word of God; if a Christian grows by the Word of God, has victory over sin, grows into sanctification and holy life through the Word; if a Christian develops faith, has answered prayer, has daily guidance, and wins souls by the blessed Word of God, then of course peace and joy will be his.

Read Psalm 119 and find how often David says that the Word of God is his delight, his joy, his praise! Remember that Jeremiah said, "Thy words were found, and I did eat them; and thy word was unto me the joy and rejoicing of mine heart: for I am called by thy name, O Lord God of hosts" (Jer. 15:16). We are told how precious are the judgments, the statutes, the law of the Lord; "more to be desired are they than gold, yea, than much fine gold: sweeter also than honey and the honeycomb" (Psa. 19:10). I pray that every reader may set out to love the Word, to live "by every word that proceedeth out of the mouth of God." Then may he come to the time when he can say like the psalmist, "Thy testimonies have I taken as an heritage for ever: for they are the rejoicing of my heart" (Psa. 119:111). How shallow is the life of a Christian who does not every day read much of the Word of God. I am shocked to find that most Christians have never even one time read the Bible through! How can they hope to have the power of God? How can they expect to have the daily victory, the soul-winning power, the joy, the peace that good Christians have? God has ordained that we should live daily by every word that proceedeth from the mouth of God.

These words will have been written in vain unless the reader sets out to master the Word of God, to read it, to know it, to memorize pages, chapters, hundreds of verses of it. If the reader simply acknowledges the truth of this doctrine but does not set out to practice the command to live by every word of the Scripture, the reader will have sinned and the message will have failed. In the name of Jesus Christ who so loved the Scriptures and who commands us to live by them all, by every word of them, I charge you to begin this very day to live in the Word of God, to meditate in the Scriptures day and night, to follow them any way they lead you, at any cost in the world; to make them your joy and delight forever!

6

What the Christian Should Do with His Bible

"Blessed is the man . . . But his delight is in the law of the Lord; and in his law doth he meditate day and night. And he shall be like a tree planted by the rivers of water, that bringeth forth his fruit in his season; his leaf also shall not wither; and whatsoever he doeth shall prosper."
—Psalm 1:1–3.

"Only be thou strong and very courageous, that thou mayest observe to do according to all the law, which Moses my servant commanded thee: turn not from it to the right hand or to the left, that thou mayest prosper whithersoever thou goest. This book of the law shall not depart out of thy mouth; but thou shalt meditate therein day and night, that thou mayest observe to do according to all that is written therein: for then thou shalt make thy way prosperous, and then thou shalt have good success."—Joshua 1:7, 8.

THE BIBLE is the greatest tangible treasure on this earth! It means more to the success and civilization and happiness and goodness of mankind than all other writings that were ever penned. The Bible is literally miraculous. I do not mean simply that it is wonderful, that it is superlative; I mean that it came into being by the supernatural work of the Holy Spirit. It is the miraculous revelation of God. The message itself is a miracle like the conception of Jesus Christ without a human father, wrought by the Holy Spirit in the womb of a virgin. The same Holy Spirit brought into being the Bible. The Bible itself is as much supernatural as the regenerated heart of a Christian wrought by the same Holy Spirit. I speak now not of the leather cover, the paper, ink and thread, but of the words and message of this Book of God. It is the greatest treasure ever seen upon earth except the Lord Jesus Himself who is also called "The Word of God" (Rev. 19:13).

It is not surprising then, that by divine inspiration we are told that to meditate day and night in the Bible in order to follow it is the perfect secret of success and prosperity in everything! Of such a Christian this Scripture plainly says, "And whatsoever he doeth shall prosper" (Psa. 1:3). And to Joshua, on this condition of meditating day and night in the Word of God in order to follow it and not depart from it, God promised, "Then thou shalt make thy way prosperous, and then thou shalt have good success."

Perfect success in everything—what a boon! Success and prosperity in health, in business, in marriage, in family life, in prayer, in soul winning, in spiritual happiness—all these and everything else good is promised the one who meditates day and night in the Word of God in order to live by it. This is so revolutionary, so far-reaching that the mind passes over the promise without grasping it. Let us say it again; the man whose delight is in the Word of God and who meditates therein day and night will never have withered leaves, will never be without fruit in season, and literally everything he does will prosper! Such is the clear, emphatic statement of the infallible Word of God!

Whatever King Midas touched turned to gold. He could have all the gold he wanted and of course could have all that gold would buy. But that legendary gift was a far lesser gift than this promised by the Word of God, for once King Midas touched his beautiful little daughter and she turned to gold. You see, the Midas-touch did not guarantee happiness. It could not bring any blessings of the heart and home besides wealth. But this promise of God is that not only in financial matters, but in everything else, the Christian is to prosper who delights in the Word of God, who meditates therein day and night, that he may follow it.

Ponce de Leon sought far and wide for the fabled Fountain of Youth. Of course he never found the water that one could drink and so retain forever youth's figure and strength and careless ease. But the Christian who takes to heart what I am telling you now about the Word of God will find a fountain greater than Ponce de Leon ever imagined! He will find the fountain which guarantees prosperity; prosperity in farm or business, prosperity in love and marriage, prosperity in rearing children, prosperity in making friends, prosperity in health and happiness, prosperity in answered prayer, in souls won, in successful ministry. In fact, here is promised prosperity and success in the life that now is and the life to come!

One may ride across the western prairies of Texas where I grew up and find usually only the scrubby mesquite, with occasional chaparral and sometimes cactus, but no trees worthy of the name. But sometimes he may see a tall winding line of big trees—cottonwood, hackberry, elm. That is the mark of a watercourse. The creek may not have water in it always, but at least here when it rains the water has run and soaked the ground and so the large trees can live and grow. In that semi-arid country, as in much of Palestine where the First Psalm was written, there is not enough moisture for large trees except by watercourses.

What a picture is this of a Christian! The Christian lives in a drought-stricken world. The Christian is not at home in this world. For a Christian, the native climate of this world does not make for growth and success and prosperity. But, thank God, there runs a river of water by which every Christian may be planted. As the Christian meditates day and night in the Word of God, "he shall be like a tree planted by the rivers of water, that bringeth forth his fruit in his season; his leaf also shall not wither; and whatsoever he doeth shall prosper." Blessed is the Christian who realizes this truth and sets all the roots of his being to soaking in the Word of God, that he may live by its wealth all the time! The Bible is to the Christian all that the water is to the tree. I promise you, on the authority of God's Word, that you may have success and happiness in the largest, fullest measure, in everything you undertake if you will set out to soak up the Word of God, to meditate in it day and night and know all its riches in order to follow all its blessed precepts!

In this message then, let us see how a Christian may receive all the blessings which are promised to one absorbed continually in the Word of God.

I. The Christian Should Diligently Read the Bible

"Blessed is he that readeth, and they that hear the words of this prophecy . . ." (Rev. 1:3). And the Apostle Paul wrote to Timothy by divine inspiration, commanding, "Give attendance to reading . . ." (I Tim. 4:13). He begged Timothy who was coming to see him in prison, "Bring . . . the books, but especially the parchments" (II Tim. 4:13).

A blessing on the one who reads and on all who hear the Word of God! We must remember that when the Bible was written printing had not been invented. Only a very small percentage of people could read; for others who could read, there were no printed books. There were only a few manuscripts laboriously and expensively copied by hand. Naturally most people never had for themselves a copy of the whole Bible nor even of one book of the Bible. They must hear the Scripture read in the church or synagogue or they must hear it quoted by those who memorized some of the beloved passages. So we may properly say, I think, that all the Scriptures which say, "Hear the word of the Lord!" or "Hearken diligently unto me . . . hear, and your soul shall live" or the words of Jesus, "He that hath ears to hear, let him hear" are solemnly commanding every person to familiarize himself with the Bible. How simple and easy this is when one may read for himself from his own Bible. So the first duty of a

Christian as regards the Bible is to *read it;* diligently, carefully, lovingly and repeatedly, to read it. Read the Bible!

First, let me say most earnestly that the Christian should read ALL of the Bible. The Christian ought to read all the genealogies, all the historical books, all the hard-to-understand prophecies. Remember that *"ALL* scripture is given by inspiration of God, and is profitable for doctrine, for reproof, for correction, for instruction in righteousness: That the man of God may be perfect, throughly furnished unto all good works" (II Tim. 3:16, 17). It is a shocking proof of spiritual immaturity that the big majority of professing Christians have never even read the Bible through one time. God has had written down for us His instructions, His comfort, His promises, His warnings, and we chose to read a little of them and ignore the rest. That is presumptuous sin.

A modernist preacher said to a Christian woman teaching the Word of God to children in his church, "Teach them the life of Christ. Don't teach them the Old Testament; there is nothing to that." His was the folly of ignorance and of unbelief, which are usually joined together. Infidels who hate the Bible and who, incidentally, hate the Christ of the Bible, like to say that there are parts of the Bible that ought to be kept from children and young people. But those are wicked words coming from wicked hearts. There are no parts of the Bible which are unfit for anybody to read who can read. There are no parts of the Bible that a child can understand but what can have only the most blessed results in his life, with proper teaching. Everybody ought to read the Bible, ought to read it all, every line, with the devotion and reverence that befits the living Word of God, God's own precious revelation to men.

The objections of those who do not read the Bible cannot stand honest investigation. Some say that many portions of the Bible are uninteresting. No, there are no uninteresting parts of the Bible; there are just uninterested people! Once, in my own private reading, I came to the genealogy of Christ in Luke 3. I found the reading monotonous; my mind had a tendency to wander and I had no relish for the reading. But as I became conscious of this state of mind I was deeply convicted. This was the very Word of God, God's precious and wonderful and living Word! I felt guilty and so confessed my sin to God. Immediately I made a resolution, "I will preach on the genealogy of Jesus Christ next Sunday morning." So I spent the week in study of that genealogy of Christ, compared with the one in Matthew 1. I asked God to give me a loving expectancy as I read the Word. I asked Him to give me an understanding heart. The Scripture which I had in my heart somewhat despised (God forgive me!) now became wonderfully sweet as I found that Jesus was indeed the Son of Man; the Son of kings and paupers, of harlots and saints, of Jews and Gentiles. My study brought a rich blessing to my own soul and the sermon on Sunday morning was received as food from Heaven for hungry hearts. It made a tremendous spiritual impact upon my congregation. There never had been anything wrong with the genealogies; there had been something wrong with my poor, cold, uninterested heart! Every Christian should find delight in Ezekiel, in Chronicles, in the minor prophets, as well as in the Psalms and the New Testament. Read it all!

"I read the Bible but I cannot understand it," says one who would excuse his sinful neglect of the Word. But that objection is not a good one. It is hardly an honest one nor an intelligent one.

To be sure, since the Bible is the fountain of all wisdom, the revelation of the infinite God, no sensible person will expect to learn all of it at once. But any Christian who reads the Bible with real delight, who meditates on it and who prays for the Spirit of God to guide him in understanding, will find the Bible the richest mine of pleasurable reading which he ever knew. Lack of interest is back of most lack of understanding. Reading and study will bring further understanding, of course, but any child of God who loves the Word can find it surpassingly, entrancingly interesting, and will find that its richest truths more and more are made clear to his heart. I have been amazed to find how even little children can understand much of the Bible. Every one of my six daughters has been accustomed to reading the Word of God aloud at the breakfast table, and we have gone through the whole Bible again and again. Little ones who have just learned to read begin to take their part in the circle in which every member of the family reads his part in turn. I have found the children learn the sense of the Scriptures.

Who is there who cannot understand the Ten Commandments and know that it is wrong to worship idols, to swear, to murder, to lie, to steal, to commit adultery, to covet? Who is there who cannot understand, "Blessed are the pure in heart" or others of the Beatitudes, or the plain instructions of the Sermon on the Mount? Who is there who cannot understand, "Let not your heart be troubled," or, "The Lord is my shepherd; I shall not want"? It is a silly excuse of an uninterested heart when people say, "I cannot understand the Bible." Of course none of us will understand it all until we awake with the Saviour, perfect and in His likeness. But it is an inexhaustible mine of wealth and joy to every honest, seeking heart who reads it.

Dr. Amos R. Wells' beautiful poem, "Read the Bible Through," says:

I SUPPOSED I knew my Bible,
  Reading piece-meal, hit or miss;
Now a bit of "John" or "Matthew,"
  Now a snatch of "Genesis."
Certain chapters of "Isaiah,"
  Certain "Psalms"—the twenty-third,
Twelfth of "Romans," first of "Proverbs."
  Yes, I thought I knew the Word.
But I found a *thorough* reading
  Was a different thing to do,
And the way was unfamiliar
  When I read the Bible *through*.
Ye who treat the Crown of Writings
  As you treat no other book—
Just a paragraph disjointed,
  Just a crude, impatient look—

Try a worthier procedure,
Try a broad and steady view;
You will kneel in very rapture
When you read the Bible THROUGH.

Yes, all of the Bible is the Word of God. It is all profitable. Every Christian should read it all many times.

There is a complaint that young people these days cannot understand the archaic English of the King James Authorized Version of the Bible. I do not believe a word of it! Again, the real reason back of the excuse is lack of interest in the Word of God. Children in grammar school learn the meaning of "thou" and "thee." I have taught high school students and college freshmen some of Shakespeare's plays which were in the same Elizabethan English as the King James Version of the Bible, but ten times as hard. These youngsters even read Chaucer, where the language is far less modern than the King James Version of the Bible. It does not take as much specialized knowledge of archaic English to understand the King James Version of the Bible as it requires specialized knowledge to read some modern comic books! People who try even moderately soon become perfectly accustomed to the language of the King James Version of the Bible and delight in the beauties of its English. Even a child could never have a better foundation for understanding fine literature and a finer appreciation of words than that gained through regular reading of the Bible.

One may, if preferred, read the American Standard Version, not the Revised Standard Version. It is a fad to read modern translations of the Bible, a fad of which Christians should beware. First, no one-man translation of the Bible is comparable in accuracy to the King James and American Standard Versions. A one-man translation necessarily has one man's interpretation on some passages. But more important, most one-man translations are by modernists. No young Christian should be trusted with the critical notes of Weymouth's Translation. Moffatt's Translation has been applauded by high-brows but it is not always true to the original manuscripts, since no modernist has the same reverence for the literal meaning of the Scripture as a Bible believer has. Phillips' *Letters to Young Churches* is not a real translation at all but a paraphrase, and sometimes an abominable parody. Williams' Translation of the New Testament is good especially on the tenses of verbs, but for general reading Christians had better stay with the King James Version or the American Standard Version, and to memorize Scriptures from these versions and teach and preach from them.

Any normal reader who loves the Word of God and reads it with a prayerful heart, can understand it. Students may have a Bible dictionary and a concordance. We especially recommend the Scofield Reference Bible because of the helps on pages where needed which greatly simplifies the study of the Bible. But the one principal way to learn the Bible is simply to read it and read it.

Dr. James M. Gray, long president of Moody Bible Institute and a noted Bible teacher, said that he had a simple plan which he always followed before teaching any portion of the Word of God. He would read it over, read it over, read it over at least five times before attempting to explain any chapter in the Word of God. He felt that it was not only unnecessary, but unwise, to go to commentaries and try to get the meaning of the Scripture from men until he had given the Scripture a chance to speak to his own attentive heart, as he read the passage repeatedly.

How much of the Scripture should a Christian read each day? Surely all will agree that the Christian ought to read the Bible, but how much of the Bible should be a normal daily portion? Once a backslidden young man came to me for help and together we prayed. He confessed his sins and his backsliding and was restored to fellowship and to joy of the Lord. Then I said to him, "Now if you would live near the Lord and have joy and happiness and strength to overcome temptation, you must set out to read the Bible."

"But I do read the Bible," he protested, "I read a verse in the Bible nearly every day!"

I replied, "You do nearly kill yourself reading the Bible, don't you?"

How shocking that anyone could think of himself as a normal and obedient Christian when reading only a verse or two of the Bible each day.

Suppose we start with the minimum thought that any young Christian should read the Bible through within a year's time. To do so he might read three chapters of the Bible on weekdays and five chapters on Sunday, thus completing the entire Bible in less than a year. Or if he should read four chapters a day—say one chapter in the New Testament or a Psalm, and three chapters of the rest of the Old Testament daily—he would read the Bible through in a little more than ten months. Surely this should be a minimum. Who is there who thinks he could be a good Christian when spending less than fifteen or thirty minutes a day with the Word of God, the source of all wisdom? How would anybody claim that he was meeting God's requirement, to delight in the law of the Lord and to meditate therein day and night, if he were not willing to spend fifteen to thirty minutes a day with the Word of God?

John Quincy Adams, sixth president of the United States, was one of the most learned men of his day. In letters to his son he repeatedly urged the son to read the Bible. He said:

> "I have myself, for many years, made it a practice to read through the Bible once every year. I have always endeavored to read it with the same spirit and temper of mind which I now recommend to you: that is, with the intention and desire that it may contribute to my advancement in wisdom and virtue. My custom is, to read four or five chapters every morning, immediately after rising from my bed. It employs about an hour of my time, and seems to me the most suitable manner of beginning the day. But, as other cares, duties, and occupations engage the remainder of it, I have perhaps never a sufficient portion of my time in meditation, upon what I have read. Every time I read the Book through, I understand some passages which I never understood before, and which I should have done, at a former reading, had it been effected with a sufficient degree of attention."

Dr. Howard A. Kelly, long professor in Johns Hopkins University, famous surgeon, scientist, author, published that for a period of more than twenty years he had spent an average of two hours a day in reading the Bible in some six languages. Dr. Kelly says in "How I Study My Bible."

> "The very best way to study the Bible is simply to read it daily with close attention and with prayer to see the light that shines from its pages, to meditate upon it, and to continue to read until somehow it works itself, its words, its expressions, its teachings, its habits of thought, and its presentation of God and His Christ into the very warp and woof of one's being. No, there is nothing remarkable about that, it is wonderfully simple. *But it works,* and one does come, in this way, to know the Bible and to understand it. What appears, to a beginner, as a great knowledge of the Bible is thus often only the natural result of a persevering use of the simplest of all methods, namely, reading the Book day by day until it becomes extremely familiar in all its parts."

Many great men of God, including Gladstone, Robert E. Lee, and the late kings George and Edward of England, read the Bible daily.

However, I feel that for most Christians who take the Bible seriously it would be better to set out to read as much of one book as possible in a day. Most of the books of the Bible can be easily read in spare time in one day, and they yield their best fruits to the reader who reads right on through with unbroken attention.

In Dallas, Texas, a good businessman was a member of the church of which I was pastor. I urged upon the people the daily reading of the Word of God until he was ashamed. So reluctantly he set out to read several chapters daily in the Bible and to read it through within a year's time. After a few days he got over in the book of Genesis, to the story of Joseph. How entranced he was with that heart-moving tale, divinely told! He sat up until the wee small hours of the morning reading the rest of the story to see how it ended. The next Sunday he said to me, "Brother Rice, why didn't somebody tell me that the Bible is like that? That is more interesting than any book of history or any novel!" And so it is if one has an interested heart and if one gives the kind of attention to the reading that is given when one reads with genuine devotion and enjoyment. So read a whole book of the Bible, if possible, at one sitting, and so become familiar with it.

A simple device I have sometimes used to make sure that I did not neglect some portions of the Word of God is that when I finished a book of the Bible I would mark lightly in pencil at the beginning of the book the day on which I finished reading it. Then as I looked through my Bible I could soon tell whether there were some books that I had not read within a year's time and I would feel under obligation to read it.

Certainly some parts of the Bible should be read over and over, more than other parts. Some verses and some chapters you will want to memorize and study in detail. But above everything else, the main requirement for learning the Bible is simply to read it, to read it over and over, to read consecutively, to read with earnest prayer and with undivided attention. Thus any earnest Christian can get a good working knowledge of the whole Bible. So read the Bible, read it all, read long passages consecutively, and read some of it every day with deepest enjoyment.

II. Christians Should Memorize Much of the Bible

"Thy word have I hid in mine heart," said the psalmist, "that I might not sin against thee" (Psa. 119:11). The Christian should hide God's Word in his heart. When Jesus was tempted of the Devil, He did not have a Bible with Him. But He had memorized many Scriptures so He could answer, to every temptation, "It is written!" It is too late to load your gun when a bear charges you. And it may be too late for one to gain the strength and courage from the Word of God to defeat Satan after temptation comes in sudden assault. The Word hidden in the heart is a constant strength against temptation. Instructions clearly memorized come in handy when one comes to a crossroad.

There are many reasons why Christians should memorize a great deal of Scripture. Bible preachers must have memorized a great many Scriptures because, of necessity, their preaching usually was done without a Bible at hand. The hand-copied manuscripts of separate books were very few and very precious. They were kept safely stored away and brought out to read in the public services, when such a manuscript was available. But Bible preachers so diligently memorized Scripture that they could preach the Word of God which they had thus hidden in their hearts.

The fathers and mothers were commanded to hide the Word of God in their hearts, both that they might live thereby and that they might teach their children the Word of God. In Deuteronomy 6:6–9 is the following enlightening command:

"And these words, which I command thee this day, shall be in thine heart: And thou shalt teach them diligently unto thy children, and shalt talk of them when thou sittest in thine house, and when thou walkest by the way, and when thou liest down, and when thou risest up. And thou shalt bind them for a sign upon thine hand, and they shall be as frontlets between thine eyes. And thou shalt write them upon the posts of thy house, and on thy gates."

Here the people of Israel were commanded to keep in their heart the words of Holy Scripture. They were commanded to "teach them diligently unto thy children." They were commanded to "talk of them when thou sittest in thine house, and when thou walkest by the way, and when thou liest down, and when thou risest up." Night and day, walking, eating, resting, godly people were to remember the Word of God, were to talk about it and explain it to their children. In that day when there were no printed Bibles any such remembering the Word of God, talking about the Word of God and teaching the Word of God to their children would necessarily involve memorized Scripture. So God says, "These words, which I command thee this day, SHALL BE IN THINE HEART."

The many commands to meditate in the Word of God necessarily involve memory work. How can one meditate on a Scripture which he has not read well enough to know the sense of it, even the words? Meditation involves previous reading and some measure of memorization.

The only way a Christian can always take the Word of God with him is to hide it in his heart, that is, learn whole passages of Scripture by memory and so always have it available for meditation. You may carry the Bible with you, but you cannot instantly find every Scripture that you ought to think about. Nor do time and circumstances allow turning, just any moment, to the Scripture itself to read afresh the passage in question, during a day's work. But Scriptures that are memorized may be sweet even to the subconscious mind. They may be there, rich and fruitful for us to enjoy at any moment we choose to turn and feast upon them and be blessed by them. Any knowledge of the Scripture is imperfect which does not involve memory work. Those portions of sacred writ which have blessed me most are those which I learned by heart.

There have been times when I was so burdened, so distraught, so harried by duties and so fatigued in mind and body that I could not consciously dig in the Word of God and study with the attention which it requires. But in such times of stress I could call to mind passages already memorized and I found that the labor was gone and the sweetness remained. I could enjoy them, feast upon them, be blessed by these passages without the labor of reading or trying to understand. Instead, they were already understood and the words were already mine and the thoughts were as fresh and sweet as ever.

How much of the Scripture should each Christian memorize? I think the average Christian should memorize many whole chapters and hundreds of verses.

In my family we have often memorized Scripture in connection with our family worship just after breakfast. Sometimes I assigned Scriptures for memorization to be reported on later, just as schools require certain work brought in after private study or preparation. We have memorized Psalms 1, 8, 15, 23, 24, 34, 37, 100, 103, 121, 126, John 3 and 14, Romans 8 and 12, I Corinthians 13, Philippians 4, and Matthew 28. We have great joy each Easter Sunday morning in quoting from memory, as a family, Matthew 28. At Christmastime we quote from memory the Christmas story as given in Luke 2. We have memorized, of course, the Beatitudes and many other passages in the Bible, as well as hundreds of verses. This Scripture memory work has been a wonderful occasion of fellowship in the home, besides the enormous blessing which the Scripture itself brings. Of course I do not believe that I have done all I ought to do in memorization of the Scripture.

However, the continual digging in the Word of God and the memorization of large portions of Scripture provide one of the richest elements in my preaching. When my daughter was writing advertising on my book of sermons, *The Ruin of a Christian,* she counted Scriptures used and found, as I recall, that I had quoted an average of thirty-eight Scripture passages per sermon. I know that Bible preaching may well be powerful preaching, and I urge every preacher to memorize, to memorize, to memorize the Word of God and make the message his own, ready on tap for quotation at any time. But every Christian, whether a preacher or not, needs to be loaded with the living Word of God for teaching, for personal soul-winning effort, for the admonition of other Christians and for the feeding of his own soul.

Let me summarize for you these compelling reasons why a Christian should memorize many, many Scriptures.

1. Scripture hidden in the heart is a safeguard against temptation. "Thy word have I hid in mine heart," said the psalmist, "that I might not sin against thee" (Psa. 119:11).

2. Only by having many Scriptures memorized can one call them to mind for use with others when occasion serves. For example, Christian parents are plainly commanded to teach their children continually the words of the Lord and to talk about them during all the routine of daily living.

3. Christians are commanded, "Be ready always to give an answer to every man that asketh you a reason of the hope that is in you" (I Pet. 3:15). A Christian should be loaded with a scriptural answer to scriptural questions. In personal soul-winning efforts one should have always available Scriptures to answer various kinds of objections. The soul winner might take the book, *Scripture Memorizing and Successful Personal Work,* by Dr. Oscar Lowry (Moody Press). Dr. R. A. Torrey's *Vest Pocket Companion for Soul Winners* is very rich to supply Scriptures that are pertinent to bring conviction, to solve difficulties, to answer objections, to bring sinners to decisions. Why not get it and set out to memorize all the Scriptures which are given so that you will be loaded with the divine message for any need that may arise?

Or it might be simpler to take my little twenty-four-page pamphlet, *"What Must I Do to Be Saved?"* and go through it and memorize all the Scriptures in it, with references. Then perhaps you should mark them in your own Bible and always be able to turn to them, or to quote them by memory instantly when needed. Good soul winners are always those who can use the Word of God effectively because they have hidden much of it in their hearts.

4. The Holy Spirit's leadership of a Christian will depend much on how much he knows of the Word of God. Jesus said, "But the Comforter, which is the Holy Ghost, whom the Father will send in my name, he shall teach you all things, and bring all things to your remembrance, whatsoever I have said unto you" (John 14:26). But how can the Holy Spirit bring to your remembrance things that Jesus said if you never learned what He said? You see, the Holy Spirit is unable to help you understand the Scripture that you do not know. If you do not know the words of it, you cannot know

the meaning of it. The Holy Spirit cannot bring to mind nor help you understand a Scripture which you never did have in your memory.

5. All the Scriptures which teach that a Christian should meditate on the Word of God necessarily imply that he should have learned the Scriptures so he could meditate upon them. Did any reader ever meditate on the Koran? Not if you never read any of the Koran nor knew what it said! Did any reader ever meditate on the Book of Mormon? Not unless you know some of the Book of Mormon! To meditate means to consider, to analyze, to muse upon some passage or truth of which you already know something. If you do not know the words you cannot meditate upon the meaning and get the meaning of the words.

III. The Christian Should Live the Bible, Follow It at Any Cost

The Saviour's scathing denunciation of the scribes and Pharisees in Matthew 23 was based on the simple but terrible accusations. They read and taught the law, but they did not keep it! They who were the public custodians of the manuscripts of the Old Testament Scriptures were familiar with the letter of the Scriptures and prided themselves not only on knowing the law, but on knowing the commentaries and traditions about the law; but they neither went into the kingdom of Heaven themselves nor suffered others to go in. They paid tithe of mint and anise and cummin, and omitted the weightier matters of the law, judgment, mercy and faith. They were blind guides, hypocrites, outwardly appearing righteous unto men. It is obvious from the example of the scribes and the Pharisees that to read the Bible, to know the Bible, even to memorize great portions of the Bible, is not enough.

These same Pharisees and scribes knew well the prophecies about the coming Messiah, but when He came they rejected the Saviour and crucified Him.

The command and promise given to Joshua was:

"Only be thou strong and very courageous, that thou mayest observe to do according to all the law, which Moses my servant commanded thee: turn not from it to the right hand or to the left, that thou mayest prosper whithersoever thou goest. This book of the law shall not depart out of thy mouth; but thou shalt meditate therein day and night, that thou mayest observe to do according to all that is written therein: for then thou shalt make thy way prosperous, and then thou shalt have good success."—Josh. 1:7, 8.

Joshua was to meditate day and night in the law, but for the express purpose, "that thou mayest observe to do according to all that is written therein." He was to "turn not from it to the right hand or to the left, that thou mayest prosper whithersoever thou goest." There is no promised prosperity for knowing the letter of the Scripture except as one follows the light of that Scripture, from the heart.

Self-will is the greatest single obstacle to understanding of the Word of God. The Lord Jesus gave the great rule concerning this in John 3:19–21:

"And this is the condemnation, that light is come into the world, and men loved darkness rather than light, because their deeds were evil. For every one that doeth evil hateth the light, neither cometh to the light, lest his deeds should be reproved. But he that doeth truth cometh to the light, that his deeds may be made manifest, that they are wrought in God."

Why do men not come to the light of the Word of God? For the same reason that men stay away from Christ Jesus, the Light of the World. They love darkness rather than light because their deeds are evil. Doing evil, they hate light and do not come to the light because the light reproves their sins. One who has self-will, or rebellion, or an idolatrous attachment to a doctrine, or a way of life that is contradicted by the Bible does not have a heart open to the Bible. But one who does what truth he knows comes to the light, willing that his deeds may be examined and made manifest by the Word of God. The honest heart that longs to do the will of God can come to the Bible with an open mind, willing to do as God says do, willing to stop doing what God says not to do. A heart fully surrendered to the will of God comes willing to accept any doctrine taught in the Word of God, willing to reject any doctrine opposed by the Word of God. Attitude of heart is the great deciding factor in whether people can be taught the truth about doctrine and life, or whether they cannot see it or will not follow it.

I do not mean that always this blindness is intentional or conscious. Men often love the Word, but perhaps they do not love it first. Men want to follow the Word, but they do not want that as badly as they want to follow their inherited denominational doctrine, or some cherished plan of life of their own. The best way to *understand* the Bible is to set the heart wholly to *obey* the Word of God; to believe the Word of God, to follow the Word of God, and live it out as God makes it clear to the believing heart. Jesus said in John 7:17, "If any man will do his will, he shall know of the doctrine, whether it be of God, or whether I speak of myself." The Revised Standard Version is clearer still, "If any man's will is to do his will, he shall know whether the teaching is from God or whether I am speaking on my own authority." Willingness to do the will of God makes it so one can know the truth. Those who rejected Christ were not willing to do the will of God. Perhaps they were blinded, but their own sinful heart attitude caused the blindness.

Romans 1 tells us that the whole heathen world became heathen, lost the knowledge of God that all the race once had "because that, when they knew God, they glorified him not as God, neither were thankful; but became vain in their imaginations, and their foolish heart was darkened" (vs. 21). Then we are told that "God also gave them up to uncleanness" (vs. 24). "God gave them up unto vile affections" (vs.

26). "God gave them over to a reprobate mind" (vs. 28). The whole race descended from godly Noah and his sons, and once knew God but because they were not willing to follow the light they had, they lost the light.

An infidel who had long denied the truth of the Bible and insisted that the rational mind could not accept many of the doctrines of the Bible, was converted in a great revival campaign, as Dr. Bob Jones tells the story. The assault of this Spirit-filled evangelist was on the man's will and conscience and was not primarily a cold matching of wits on the intellectual plane. The unbeliever, deeply convicted of his sins, surrendered to Christ and then told the evangelist, "When I took the first step out into the aisle to confess Christ as my Saviour, every doubt I ever had fled away!" The infidel may have been sincere about his doubts, but they were nevertheless the result of a wrong heart attitude. He would not previously come to Christ in his heart, and that left his mind darkened to the truth.

D. L. Moody tells how a woman said to him, "I do not see anything wrong in the theater, in dancing and cards. You will have to explain what is wrong with these things to me before I will quit them." The great evangelist wisely told the woman, "First come to Jesus Christ and put your trust in Him. Then I promise you I will explain all these things to you honestly and fully." But when she came to Christ and trusted Him as Saviour, she suddenly knew what was wrong with these sinful practices and needed no further explanation. I am saying that one cannot understand the Bible without a heart that is surrendered to do the will of God. Why should God explain His rich secrets to those who do not love Him enough to follow Him? Why should God make His will plain for those who will not do it when they know it?

I wonder if the reader is really eager to know the will of God in his life, whatever it may cost him? Luther Rice and Adoniram Judson together had received a great vision of the need for foreign missions and had surrendered themselves to the call of God for foreign missionary work. So, with some support, they went out, hoping to do missionary work in India.

Luther Rice sailed on one boat, and Adoniram Judson on another. The long weeks at sea gave them time to study the Word of God. Each of them knew of the work of William Carey, the English Baptist in India, and they knew they would face the problem of this form of baptism. Both were pedo-Baptists, and the only support promised was from pedo-Baptist sources. Yet each of these godly missionaries who had been willing to give up home and country and comforts and, if need be, life itself for the Lord, with an openhearted study of the Bible came to the conclusion that Bible baptism should be by immersion and of believers only instead of unconverted babies. When they met on the coasts of Asia, Judson went on to Burma but Rice must return to America to organize support among the Baptists.

I am not here arguing the question of the mode of baptism. I am illustrating the fact that one cannot really learn the will of God until his heart is open to try to do the blessed will of God.

Years ago I became deeply burdened to have the fullness of the Spirit, to have the mighty power of God on my ministry and on my personal soul-winning efforts. I knew that Bible Christians had this mighty power of God. I knew that D. L. Moody, Charles G. Finney, R. A. Torrey, and other great soul winners had a special enduement of power from on high. With long years of study and with much prayer I know that God has helped me to understand the Bible doctrine of the fullness of the Spirit. And I assure you that with great heart-searching I promised God I would go anywhere, accept any doctrine, join any group to which the blessed Word of God plainly led me. With all my heart I searched the Word of God to find if God had promised the eradication of the carnal nature and sinless perfection. I could not find it in the Bible. With all my heart I searched to see if I should look for the sign of speaking with tongues. I read the best books on the subject from all sources. I attended the services of good people of many faiths, including those who talked in tongues. But all the time my heart cried out to God that I would not take anything except what I found in the Word of God as authoritative. I told Him that I would go anywhere this blessed Book led me! And I feel I have a right to full assurance that God did lead me because my heart sought His power, for His purposes and to carry out His soul-winning command, and because I was willing to suffer any ostracism, any embarrassment, any reproach that might come upon me in order to have the power of God. I had no right to expect God to reveal His Word to me and to help me to understand except as I was willing to follow the Word of God anywhere it led me.

A man with a dirty habit told me that he did not want his wife nor children to follow his example. He thought it would be wrong for them but said about himself simply, "I will not quit it because I am not convicted in my heart." He would not hear what the Bible said about the body as the temple of the Holy Spirit and about doing all things to the glory of God, and that "whatsoever is not of faith is sin" (Rom. 14:23), and he did not feel convicted in his heart. The trouble is that his heart was not willing to be convicted by the Bible.

A woman told me that she felt a certain doctrine was right because she felt impressed that way. She was not willing to listen to the Word of God and she evaded the Scripture and explained away the Scripture to fit her belief.

Will the reader excuse another personal illustration? After I had joined the Masonic lodge, had my first three degrees paid for by kindly friends, when I hardly knew that there were preachers who actively opposed lodge membership for Christians, I found that the Bible clearly forbade the yoking up of Christians with unbelievers (II Cor. 6:14–18). I found that the Bible plainly says, "Swear not at all" (Matt. 5:34) and again, "Above all things, my brethren, swear not" (Jas.

5:12). I left the lodges because I wanted to go anywhere the Bible commanded.

How often I must have failed to have this proper heart attitude, failed to have a willingness, an eagerness to go anywhere the Bible leads, to do anything the Bible commands, to leave anything the Bible commands me to leave! But I know that heart attitude is absolutely essential to a full understanding of the Word of God and the will of God and I earnestly pray, with all my heart, that I may have this attitude.

IV. The Christian Should Meditate Day and Night in the Word of God

A Christian should read his Bible, should memorize much of the Bible, should follow the Bible and obey it at any cost; and he should meditate in the Scriptures day and night. Strangely enough, the Scripture seems to give more emphasis to meditation in the Word of God than in reading it, learning it or obeying it. The "blessed" man of Psalm 1 who is promised that "whatsoever he doeth shall prosper" has that supreme promise because "his delight is in the law of the Lord; and in his law doth he meditate day and night."

Joshua was commanded, "This book of the law shall not depart out of thy mouth; but thou shalt meditate therein day and night, that thou mayest observe to do according to all that is written therein: for then thou shalt make thy way prosperous, and then thou shalt have good success." Here again, meditation in the law of the Lord is given as the only sure way that Joshua could really "observe to do according to all the law," and receive the perfect prosperity and success which was promised.

Timothy was commanded to give attendance to reading, to exhortation, to doctrine and to the gift that he had received, and to "meditate upon these things; give thyself wholly to them; that thy profiting may appear to all" (I Tim. 4:13–15). Reading and the study of doctrine was important, but the crowning blessing from the Word of God comes only to those who meditate on the Word of God.

One may read the Bible and get it in his head but not in his heart. One may read and even memorize much of the Scriptures and get the letter but not the Spirit. One may even set out to obey the Bible and become a moral man, a Pharisee, without becoming a child of God. Who is there who so devoutly tries to obey the Word of God as did unconverted John Wesley before his heart was warmed with saving faith at Aldersgate? Who more carefully and earnestly strove to obey the Word of God and to please God than did Martin Luther, the learned monk, before he came to know in his heart that "the just shall live by faith"? No one can really please God in his attitude toward the Bible, in his knowledge of the Bible, in obedience to the Bible except as, with all his heart, he learns to meditate and feed upon the Word, delighting in the Word, lovingly opening his heart to the teaching of the Holy Spirit through the Word.

George Muller, wonderful man of prayer, found that Bible meditation the first part of the day led to joy, happiness, fellowship with God and spiritual, successful prayer. In his Narratives of the Lord's dealing, Muller says,

> "It has pleased the Lord to teach me a truth, the benefit of which I have not lost for more than fourteen years. The point is this: I saw more clearly than ever that the first great primary business to which I ought to attend every day was, to have my soul happy in the Lord. The first thing to be concerned about was not how much I might serve the Lord, or how I might glorify the Lord; but how I might get my soul into a happy state, and how my inner man might be nourished. For I might seek to set the truth before the unconverted, I might seek to benefit believers, I might seek to relieve the distressed, I might in other ways seek to behave myself as it becomes a child of God in this world; and yet, not being happy in the Lord, and not being nourished and strengthened in my inner man day by day, all this might not be attended to in a right spirit. Before this time my practice had been, at least for ten years previously, as an habitual thing, to give myself to prayer after having dressed myself in the morning. Now, I saw that the most important thing I had to do was to give myself to the reading of the Word of God, and to meditation on it, that thus my heart might be comforted, encouraged, warned, reproved, instructed; and that thus, by means of the Word

of God, whilst meditating on it, my heart might be brought into experimental communion with the Lord.

"I began therefore to meditate on the New Testament from the beginning early in the morning. The first thing I did, after having asked in a few words the Lord's blessing upon His precious Word, was to begin to meditate on the Word of God, searching as it were into every verse to get blessing out of it; not for the sake of the public ministry of the Word, not for the sake of preaching on what I had meditated upon, but for the sake of obtaining food for my own soul. The result I have found to be almost invariably this, that after a very few minutes my soul has been led to confession, or to thanksgiving, or to intercession, or to supplication; so that, though I did not, as it were, give myself to prayer, but to meditation, yet it turned almost immediately more or less into prayer. When thus I have been for a while making confession or intercession or supplication, or have given thanks, I go on to the next words or verse, turning all, as I go on, into prayer for myself or others, as the Word may lead to it, but still continually keeping before me that food for my own soul is the object of my meditation. The result of this is, that there is always a good deal of confession, thanksgiving, supplication, or intercession mingled with my meditation, and that my inner man almost invariably is ever sensibly nourished and strengthened, and that by breakfast time, with rare exceptions, I am in a peaceful if not happy state of heart. Thus also the Lord is pleased to communicate unto me that which, either very soon after or at a later time, I have found to become food for other believers, though it was not for the sake of the public ministry of the Word that I gave myself to meditation, but for the profit of my own inner man."

The best understanding of the Bible, the best guidance, light, strength, and growth of the Christian, cannot be wrought by the Bible except as one lovingly meditates on the Word of God.

This is one of the reasons that the Bible is not really learned in the classroom. Real knowledge of the Bible is a heart matter. God commands, "And these words, which I command thee this day, shall be *in thine heart*" (Deut. 6:6). David said, "Thy word have I hid *in mine heart,* that I might not sin against thee" (Psa. 119:11). David prayed the Lord, "Incline *my heart* unto thy testimonies, and not to covetousness" (Psa. 119:36).

The divinely-inspired words of the psalmist about the Bible are words of the emotion. "I have rejoiced in the way of thy testimonies," "I will delight myself in thy statutes," "Make me to go in the path of thy commandments; for therein do I delight." And again, "And I will delight myself in thy commandments, which I have loved." These quotations are in Psalm 119; and there again is the statement, "But I will keep thy precepts with my whole heart"; and again, "But I delight in thy law." The psalmist said: "How sweet are thy words unto my taste! yea, sweeter than honey to my mouth!" (Psa. 119:103). He said: "Thy testimonies have I taken as an heritage for ever: for they are the rejoicing of my heart" (vs. 111). Read that longest chapter in the Bible, Psalm 119, and there you will find that the inspired prophet loved the law, delighted in the law, wept over the Scripture, and hoped in the Word of God. Love is a heart-word; hope is a heart-word; tears and weeping are from the heart. All these are terms of one who meditates in the blessed Word of God, who holds the words in his heart like treasured sentences and affectionate terms of endearment from a loved one.

When I was a boy hardly six years old my mother went to Heaven, but I have so often meditated over my mother's last words that I can still see her face, I can hear her asking for the song, "How Firm a Foundation." I can remember just how she looked up gladly to say, "I can see Jesus and my baby now." I say, those words are very dear, and so I have meditated on them often. That is the way God wants us to feel about His Word. The Scripture should be our delight. For it we should have deep longing; we should praise God for it, and weep because we have failed to observe God's commands. We should hope in all the promises. We should enrich our hearts and minds, saying over and over to ourselves the sweet words of the Bible.

I am saying that meditation is a heart matter. Therefore, it is more than study. One ought to study the Bible, but I have known men to study the Bible and not even know what it meant to be born again. I have known people to memorize many, many Scriptures and still think that baptism was essential to salvation, and that a good life would bring one to God. Only when one takes the Scripture into his heart and chews it, and digests it, and loves it, and submits his emotions to it, does he really get the complete benefit of the Scriptures.

The cow grazes on the green grass and fills her stomach. Then she lies down in the shade, switches her tail and chews the cud. What really happens is that she brings up from her stomach the partially-chewed grass, and chews it deliberately and thoroughly until the digestive juices can have their way perfectly with the food. Eating the grass may be like reading the Bible, or memorizing it. But chewing the cud is like the meditation which God requires of a Christian if he is to receive the full blessing of the Word of God.

Since this meditation upon the Word of God is a heart matter, one should put it first. Give God and the Bible the place above everybody else and all other books. I suggest that there is wonderful profit in taking time early in the morning, right at the opening of the doors of day, to read and meditate in the Word of God and to let the Bible itself lead us into prayer, confession, consecration and adoration.

Ralph S. Cushman well says:

I met God in the morning
When the day was at its best,
And His presence came like sunrise,
Like a glory within my breast.

All day long the presence lingered,
All day long He stayed with me,
And we sailed in perfect calmness
O'er a very troubled sea.

Other ships were blown and battered,
Other ships were sore distressed,
But the winds that seemed to drive them
Brought to us a peace and rest!

Then I thought of other mornings,
With a keen remorse of mind,
When I too had loosed the moorings,
With the Presence left behind.

So I think I know the secret,
Learned from many a troubled way;
You must seek Him in the morning
If you want Him through the day.

So one should find God in His Word in the morning.

I pray that this truth may become clear to the reader. We may believe the Bible, read the Bible, try to obey the Bible, but we are not good Christians until we learn to love the Bible; until it is sweet and precious as food; until it is like honey in the honeycomb; until it becomes like the richest mine of gold. To read the Bible from duty is good. But to read the Bible from love and with deep enjoyment is infinitely better! Oh, may God give us a heart to delight in His Word and to meditate therein day and night!

For many years I have slept with a Bible by my bedside. Poor and weak as I am, I have learned to love the precious Word of God. Often in times of stress I have reached over to the bedside table in the dark, have taken the Bible and slipped it under my pillow as a symbol that I rest my head, my burdens, and my future all in the hands of the good God. Sometimes I have taken it in my arms in the night and hugged it to my bosom and so have gone to sleep. God help us to love the Bible!

V. The Christian Should Use the Blessed Word of God Daily

How much the Bible is to the Christian! It is meat, it is bread, it is light, it is water, it is a sword, it is seed. It is a hammer. It is a fire! Blessed is the Christian who not only reads the Bible and memorizes much of it, and tries to follow it; who not only meditates in it and loves it, but who uses the Bible day by day.

First of all, the Christian should use the Word of God on himself. He should come to the Bible for cleansing. He should come to the Bible for daily encouragement. He should learn from the Bible how to live. He should receive from the Bible instructions in prayer. He should build his faith by the Word of God. He should make his appeal to God on the basis of definite promises in the Book. The Christian should use the Bible to develop spiritual wisdom, to grow in grace, and otherwise to make himself the Christian that he ought to be. Use the Bible on yourself.

The Christian also should use the Bible to teach others God's way. One who is taught should teach others. One of the best ways to really learn the Bible is to pass on what you know, and see it work its blessed results in the lives of others. Parents are to teach the Bible to the children (Deut. 6:6, 7). Husbands are to teach it to their wives (I Cor. 14:34, 35). Pastors are to teach the Word of God to their people. The Bible, Bible doctrines and facts ought to be a choice subject of conversation between the people of God. When Christians get together they should quote to each other the Scriptures, they should each learn from the other and so edify one another with the Word of God. Christian, use the Bible to teach others.

And then a Christian should use the blessed Word of God to win souls. The sower who went forth to sow good seed, in the parable Jesus told, was sowing the Word of God (Luke 8:11). Psalm 126:5 and 6 tells us, "They that sow in tears shall reap in joy. He that goeth forth and weepeth, bearing precious seed, shall doubtless come again with rejoicing, bringing his sheaves with him." The soul winner must go after sinners, he must go with a broken heart into which the Holy Spirit has wrought the compassion of Christ. But he must go with the Word of God. It takes Scripture to win souls. And those who are saved are "born again, not of corruptible seed, but of incorruptible, by the word of God, which liveth and abideth for ever" (I Pet. 1:23).

I suggest that every Christian find the Scriptures that answer the objections of sinners. Find the Scriptures that God can use to bring conviction of sin. Get acquainted with the Scriptures and use the Scriptures which make plain the plan of salvation. Use the Word of God to bring people to trust in Jesus Christ for salvation.

A Christian can be a good Christian only in proportion as he comes to know and love and follow, from his heart and not only from his head, the blessed Word of God. And before you leave this message, I beg you to consider again that one whose delight is in the law of the Lord and meditates therein day and night shall have the promised blessing of Psalm 1:1–3. His leaves will never wither, he will bring forth fruit in his season, "and whatsoever he doeth shall prosper." Blessed promise of certain and complete prosperity to everyone who meditates day and night and delights in the Word of God!

7

David and Bath-sheba

"And it came to pass, after the year was expired, at the time when kings go forth to battle, that David sent Joab, and his servants with him, and all Israel; and they destroyed the children of Ammon, and besieged Rabbah. But David tarried still at Jerusalem. And it came to pass in an eveningtide, that David arose from off his bed, and walked upon the roof of the king's house: and from the roof he saw a woman washing herself; and the woman was very beautiful to look upon. And David sent and enquired after the woman. And one said, Is not this Bath-sheba, the daughter of Eliam, the wife of Uriah the Hittite? And David sent messengers, and took her; and she came in unto him, and he lay with her; for she was purified from her uncleanness: and she returned unto her house. And the woman conceived, and sent and told David, and said, I am with child. And David sent to Joab, saying, Send me Uriah the Hittite. And Joab sent Uriah to David. And when Uriah was come unto him, David demanded of him how Joab did, and how the people did, and how the war prospered. And David said to Uriah, Go down to thy house, and wash thy feet. And Uriah departed out of the king's house, and there followed him a mess of meat from the king. But Uriah slept at the door of the king's house with all the servants of his lord, and went not down to his house. And when they had told David, saying, Uriah went not down unto his house, David said unto Uriah, Camest thou not from thy journey? why then didst thou not go down unto thine house? And Uriah said unto David, The ark, and Israel, and Judah, abide in tents; and my lord Joab, and the servants of my lord, are encamped in the open fields; shall I then go into mine house, to eat and to drink, and to lie with my wife? as thou livest, and as thy soul liveth,

I will not do this thing. And David said to Uriah, Tarry here to day also, and tomorrow I will let thee depart. So Uriah abode in Jerusalem that day, and the morrow. And when David had called him, he did eat and drink before him; and he made him drunk: and at even he went out to lie on his bed with the servants of his lord, but went not down to his house. And it came to pass in the morning, that David wrote a letter to Joab, and sent it by the hand of Uriah. And he wrote in the letter, saying, Set ye Uriah in the forefront of the hottest battle, and retire ye from him, that he may be smitten, and die. And it came to pass, when Joab observed the city, that he assigned Uriah unto a place where he knew that valiant men were. And the men of the city went out, and fought with Joab: and there fell some of the people of the servants of David; and Uriah the Hittite died also. Then Joab sent and told David all the things concerning the war."—II Samuel 11:1–18.

I DARE NOT close this book on *What It Costs to Be a Good Christian* without showing what sin does to the Christian or to anybody else. It is not common, in these days of timid preachers, in these days when the men who ought to be ministers and prophets of God are often "dumb dogs, they cannot bark" (Isa. 56:10), to hear sermons on David's scarlet sin. It is not often these days that preachers obey the injunction of Isaiah 58:1, "Cry aloud, spare not, lift up thy voice like a trumpet, and show my people their transgression, and the house of Jacob their sins." Yet I recall that in Southwestern Baptist Theological Seminary the beloved Dr. Jeff D. Ray, professor of homiletics, made us, his ministerial students, prepare sermon outlines on David's sin with Bathsheba, his shameful murder of Uriah, her husband, and the fearful consequences of this sin. Here, he said, were all the elements for great preaching. Intense human interest, a heart-moving drama, the thrilling pace of the narrative, the unutterable pathos of the outcome, and God's wonderful mercy and forgiveness—all these are themes that ought to bring out the very best in any preacher, and ought to appeal to any congregation. I am surprised and a little ashamed that I do not recall preaching more than two complete sermons on this bit of Scripture in a ministry of thirty years.

Some may feel that there is a frankness, an embarrassing forthrightness in this Scripture telling of adultery which ought not to be read or discussed from the pulpit. They are utterly mistaken, for II Timothy 3:16, 17 tells us: "All Scripture is given by inspiration of God, and is profitable for doctrine, for reproof, for correction, for instruction in righteousness: That the man of God may be perfect, throughly furnished unto all good works." The man of God ought to use this Scripture which is so profitable for reproof, correction and instruction in righteousness. This Scripture is part of the complete equipment of the man of God to promote good works among his hearers and repentance among sinners. I pray that a thousand preachers may preach on this Scripture soon. How badly the message is needed in America today!

Every child of God should feel deeply warned and should fervently take to heart the lesson of David's sin. If such a mighty Christian as David fell into such terrible sin, with what fear and trembling ought all of us walk before God and to flee temptation! Sinners and saints alike ought to face with solemn examination and with holy vows the terrible fact here emphasized, that covered-up sin leads to yet worse sin, to shameful public exposure, and to fearful punishment from God. All the Scriptures on this subject emphasize again such texts as, "Be sure your sin will find you out" (Num. 32:23); "Be not deceived; God is not mocked: for whatsoever a man soweth, that shall he also reap" (Gal. 6:7, 8); "Then when lust hath conceived, it bringeth forth sin: and sin, when it is finished, bringeth forth death" (Jas. 1:15). What solemn warning there is for all of us in the Scriptures concerning David's horrible sin and its consequences!

I. The Man Who Sinned

The prominence which God gave to David and David's great spiritual development emphasizes all the more the horrible nature of his sin and make him all the more a startling example of what can happen to a Christian who does not beware.

First, even before David was anointed to be king over Israel, Samuel was inspired to say of him: "The Lord hath sought him a man after his own heart, and the Lord hath commanded him to be captain over his people . . ." (I Sam. 13:14). David was, in a peculiar sense, a man after God's own heart. That is, he was not only a regenerated man but a man peculiarly surrendered to God, a man anxious to do the will of God, a man who the most of his life was filled with the Holy Spirit.

When David was anointed by Samuel, we are told, "And the Spirit of the Lord came upon David from that day forward" (I Sam. 16:13). As a usual thing David consistently asked God for leadership in all his enterprises. He publicly gave God the glory for his victories. God held David up as an example to Solomon, saying unto him, "And if thou wilt walk in my ways, to keep my statutes and my commandments, as thy father David did walk, then I will lengthen thy days" (I Kings 3:14). Then later the Lord sadly reports that in Solomon's old age he loved and married heathen women and followed after their gods. "For it came to pass, when Solomon was old, that his wives turned away his heart after other gods: and his heart was not perfect with the Lord his God, as was the heart of David his father" (I Kings 11:4). Here we may see how God rates David. He was the man 'whose heart was perfect with the Lord his God.' And all the kings of Judah thereafter are judged by the Lord on the basis of whether or not they followed the Lord as did David. For example, the Scripture says of Abijam, the son of Rehoboam, "Three years reigned he in Jerusalem. . . . And he walked in all the sins of his father, which he had done before him: and his heart was not perfect with the Lord his God, as the heart of David his father."

This one horrible sin of David's mars an otherwise glorious record.

Remember that even before this sin of David's God had allowed him to begin the kingly dynasty which will end in the reign of Christ on David's throne at Jerusalem. To David, God said, "And thine house and thy kingdom shall be established for ever before thee: thy throne shall be established for ever" (II Sam. 7:16). So Jesus is the "son of David." He is "the king of the Jews." And the angel Gabriel told Mary, ". . . and the Lord God shall give unto him the throne of his father David: and he shall reign over the house of Jacob for ever; and of its kingdom there shall be no end" (Luke 1:32, 33). The Lord Jesus must return to earth to sit on that throne and establish that kingdom for which we pray in the Lord's Prayer when we say, "Thy kingdom come, thy will be done on earth as it is in heaven." How great was the honor given David, the man after God's own heart!

We must remember, too, that David was not only king, but also a prophet of God. In Acts 2:29, 30 we have the inspired words of Peter about David, saying:

> *"Men and brethren, let me freely speak unto you of the patriarch David, that he is both dead and buried, and his sepulchre is with us unto this day. Therefore being a prophet, and knowing that God had sworn with an oath to him, that of the fruit of his loins, according to the flesh, he would raise up Christ to sit on his throne."*

By divine inspiration David wrote many wonderful Psalms. In these Psalms he foretold again and again the coming of Jesus, His death on the cross, salvation by His substitutionary death for sinners, and His wonderful future kingdom on earth.

When David sinned, it was a spiritual giant who sinned. When the man after God's own heart fell into adultery and murder, it was as shocking as sin could be. And who are you who read this that you do not tremble at the thought? The most anointed and powerful preacher, the most spiritual and modest Christian woman ought to search every heart motive, ought to flee fearfully from sin, since David, so great and good man of God, fell into such fearful sin!

II. The Factors in David's Sin

A licentious and wicked man, whose companions are immoral, whose past is shameful, and whose heart does not know nor love God, might fall at one step into adultery and murder; but not so David! A man so pure in heart, so fervent in his love for God, so anointed as a prophet of God, fell into the most horrible of his sins only as the climax of a series of steps. David failed in little things and then he failed in great things. James 1:14, 15 says:

> *"But every man is tempted, when he is drawn away of his own lust, and enticed. Then when lust hath conceived, it bringeth forth sin: and sin, when it is finished, bringeth forth death."*

So sin progresses in the steps of innate lust, enticement, the conception of intentional sin, and then the wages of sin, death.

What were the contributing factors in David's horrible sin?

Perhaps the first thing that led to David's sin was *idleness.* It was the time of the year when kings go forth to battle. "David sent Joab, and his servants with him, and all Israel; and they destroyed the children of Ammon, and besieged Rabbah. But David tarried still at Jerusalem" (II Sam. 11:1). The war with the Ammonites was not of David's seeking. The preceding chapter tells how David sent messengers to comfort the king of Ammon concerning the death of his father, David's friend. The king of Ammon, Hanun, took David's servants and shaved off half their beards, cut off their garments in the middle and sent them, half naked and ashamed, back to David! Then the king of Ammon enlisted the Syrians to help him and attacked David and the children of Israel. We cannot blame David for the war. But if it were right for Joab and all the servants of David to be out in the war, then it seems that David should have been there, too, doing his part. He would never have fallen into such fearful sin had he not tarried at Jerusalem idly, when others who loved him imperiled their lives for him.

The servants of David mentioned here doubtless included the thirty-seven mighty men of war named in II Samuel 23:8–39. And the last of the thirty-seven mentioned is Uriah the Hittite. All these men, with thousands of lesser soldiers, risked their lives for David. But he idled in the palace and stole the wife of one of these men who was willing to die for him!

Not all of us can be soldiers. But, oh, how careful we ought to be not to sin against other soldiers who risk their lives for us and our country. I do not believe that soldiers who come out of the service unharmed should demand pensions nor receive undue favoritism in other matters. But it is unspeakably shameful for a civilian to steal the wife of a man absent in the service of his country.

Idleness leads to sin. Idleness is probably the greatest single factor in the youthful delinquency. There is character-building discipline in work. None of us want slave labor, nor oppression of children. Every child ought to have a fair chance at a common school education. But to be overworked is not nearly so bad as to be underworked. Blessed is the child who early learns to do hard work, to keep regular hours, to earn part of his own way, to save and use money.

Fond mothers and doting fathers do their children irreparable harm just here. What a boy needs to learn in order to be a good man is to work and obey orders. What a girl needs to learn is the same lesson—honest work, a carrying of one's own responsibilities faithfully, and obedience to those in authority.

I remember a whimsical and delightful bit from a message by Dr. Bob Jones, Sr. He said the following:

> "Young man, have you been going with one of these painted dolls who lets her mother do all the work? Have you been keeping company with a girl who does not get up in time for breakfast, who leaves it to mother to wash the dishes while she spends all her time on looking pretty and pleasing herself? If she one day tells you that she likes you very much and admires you but someway she simply cannot love you and that she will always be just your good friend: and if you hear soon thereafter that she is engaged to marry another man, don't you play the fool and go and kill yourself! No, go buy them a wedding present! And don't be stingy; make it a thank offering! Then get down on your knees and thank God that He saved you from marrying a parasite who never learned to work and who could not make a good wife because she was not a good woman."

O David, David! How often you must have wished you had not idled at home and fallen into such sin while others were risking their lives for you!

Another factor that contributed greatly to David's fall was the fact that he was a king, and so exempt from the authority of others. He probably felt that he did not have to obey the law. When he looked down from his roof-top and saw his neighbor's wife bathing in the patio which was safely enclosed from all prying eyes except one who might be on the palace roof-top, David had no fear that he would be arrested as a "peeping Tom"! He was the king. And "the king can do no wrong."

Let us face it frankly, then. The higher the position one attains, the more severe are the temptations. Every man who reaches a place of eminence, a place of authority or leadership, ought more strictly and rigorously to set a watch upon his lips and keep his heart with all diligence. The more one is free from accountability to others, the more he is accountable to God. The more one is free from the control of others, the more he is tempted to sin! Young people sometimes fret at chaperones. But chaperones keep people from sin. Young people often long for the time to come when they can have their own way. They do not know it, but one day they will see that strict rearing and enforced obedience to authority were the greatest safeguards to keep them from ruin.

It is said that Vice-President Chester A. Arthur, when elected as the teammate of President Garfield was a playboy, and was counted the tool of selfish interests who sought to use him for bad ends in the government. But on the death of President Garfield, Chester A. Arthur suddenly found himself president. And with commendable integrity he suddenly broke away from all the men who would have used him for evil purposes and dedicated himself to the business of being an upright president. He was never a great president nor a great man, but he was greatly sobered by the responsibility thrust upon him so unexpectedly; and he felt the need to watch his step and safeguard every action since he was exalted to such a responsible place.

Every evangelist anointed of God and greatly used in preaching before big congregations will find that the hearts of multitudes are given into his hands. He can lead them right or wrong. How earnestly, then, should he seek the will of God and how holily should he seek to humble his heart and avoid the sins that come with prominence. Every attractive gospel singer will have foolish young women throwing themselves at his head. Unless he walks very softly and discreetly he will fall into grievous sin. The man who reaches a responsible place of importance and fame must watch his step. He will be tempted all the more, as King David was.

But a more important element even yet in David's downfall was this fact: he dallied with sin. He did not immediately resist the Devil and flee from temptation.

Do you believe that David, when he went on the palace roof to sit under the stars that eveningtide, immediately intended to go into adultery and murder? Certainly not! And when he saw the woman bathing herself in the courtyard or patio next door and below him that night after bedtime, do you think he planned at once his sin? I do not think so. First, he gazed upon the woman, another man's wife, and enjoyed her beauty, though he had no right to do it. The first glance was an accident for which David could not be blamed. But when he sat and enjoyed her beauty, the beauty of an unclothed wife of another man, it was sin.

As David looked upon her, there was first enjoyment, then desire. Then David called a servant and inquired who the woman was and was told: "Is not this Bath-sheba, the daughter of Eliam, the wife of Uriah the Hittite?" You see, David did not even know who the woman was. He did not know until this moment that her husband was away in the wars. Now the enticement of lust conceives the sin. Who is to stop him? The husband is not at home! So he sends for the woman and has her brought to meet him.

It is hard for me to believe that David even then intended to commit adultery. Perhaps he did. I think rather that he followed the impulse of the moment, and went on with the delightful temptation, letting it lead him whither it would. To be sure it was past bedtime, but he was the king and there would be no one to call him to account for an improper visit with another man's wife. And when he found her attractive, and perhaps greatly flattered by the king's attention; and young and lonely, David went on with his sin.

How much better if David, on the housetop, seeing for the first time the scene of a woman bathing next door, had risen at once and returned to his bedroom. He should have said to himself, "That is another man's wife. The man is a friend of mine, a loyal servant. I have no right to the other man's wife. I have wives of my own. I am God's man; I must not do wrong." David should have fled from the temptation at once. But dallying and tarrying, he was overwhelmed and led into sin.

David should have followed the example of Joseph down in Egypt. When Potiphar's wife caught him by his garment, saying, "Lie with me," then Joseph "left his garment in her hand, and fled, and got him out." Joseph was not only pure; he was also wise. Joseph was not only innocent; he was strong! O Christian, what a sin it is to dally around places and around people, and with habits or amusements that will lead us into damning and killing sin! Paul wrote to young Timothy, "Flee also youthful lusts" (II Tim. 2:22). The girl who goes to the dances but will not dance because it is against her conscience, will soon find that her conscience changes with her environment. She only wants to be with her crowd, perhaps, and is determined she will not follow their sins; but before long she finds herself giving way to their sins. Before long she will soothe her conscience and allow her body to be fondled and her evil nature aroused and tempted with all the lewdness that naturally follows the modern dance and the necking party.

Young people who will not drink beer and cocktails, but who get their Coca-Colas at the same fountain where beer is served, will most likely soon be drinking the intoxicants which make drunkards—and much more—of all who follow that way!

Christians who play bridge but who have a conscience against gambling will soon find out that their conscience adjusts itself to their company and soon they would rather play for stakes than embarrass a hostess, and gambling will not seem as bad as offending their worldly companions. Those who dally with sin fall into the depths.

Happy is the girl who blushes and withdraws from the immodest touch. Happy is the young man who fears the jingle of tainted money, the rustle of unholy skirts, the maddening demon of the alcoholic glass! O Christian, if you would keep your purity and your convictions, if you would avoid falling into terrible sins, then you must hate the appearances of evil and flee from youthful lusts. You must not dally with temptation if you would be victorious. David looked too long, and he lost!

Pope says, in his *Essay on Man*,

> Vice is a monster of so frightful mien
> As, to be hated, needs but to be seen.
> Yet seen too oft, familiar with her face,
> We first endure and then pity, and then embrace.

Oh, do not dally with sin if you would escape it!

But I must emphasize another element in David's fall into terrible sin. David, I fear, forgot the enemy within! He forgot his own tendency to sin. The inborn sinful nature contributed to David's fall.

He seems to have meditated much on this later. In his penitential prayer in the fifty-first Psalm, verse 5, David prayed, "Behold, I was shapen in iniquity; and in sin did my mother conceive me." That prayer was written after his sin with Bath-sheba. He was now conscious of the awful wickedness of his own natural heart.

And I am impressed that David probably saw later that he had too long ignored this carnal nature within. He had not watched himself as carefully as he might. For in the following verse, Psalm 51:6, he said, "Behold, thou desirest truth in the inward parts: and in the hidden part thou shalt make me to know wisdom." Evidently there had been some neglect of prayer, some letting down of the bars on minor matters. David had not watched and prayed as much as he ought. He had not been continually conscious of his own weakness and his own natural tendencies to evil. Now when some great temptation came, David found himself falling. He had not sufficiently safeguarded himself against his own natural weakness.

Paul the apostle was conscious that when a man is a lost sinner he has a wicked nature inherited from Adam and Eve and all his foreparents. Then when the man is saved, he has two natures, the old nature and the new. There is a part of him that is born of God and cannot sin, a part of him that is a partaker of the divine nature. But every Christian still has the old nature, too. And that struggle between the two natures is what Paul wrote about in Romans 7:14–25:

"For we know that the law is spiritual: but I am carnal, sold under sin. For that which I do I allow not: for what I would, that do I not; but what I hate, that do I. If then I

do that which I would not, I consent unto the law that it is good. Now then it is no more I that do it, but sin that dwelleth in me. For I know that in me (that is, in my flesh,) dwelleth no good thing: for to will is present with me; but how to perform that which is good I find not. For the good that I would I do not: but the evil which I would not, that I do. Now if I do that I would not, it is no more I that do it, but sin that dwelleth in me. I find then a law, that, when I would do good, evil is present with me. For I delight in the law of God after the inward man: But I see another law in my members, warring against the law of my mind, and bringing me into captivity to the law of sin which is in my members. O wretched man that I am! who shall deliver me from the body of this death? I thank God through Jesus Christ our Lord. So then with the mind I myself serve the law of God; but with the flesh the law of sin."

Paul never forgot that old carnal nature within him. In I Corinthians 9:27 he said: "But I keep under my body, and bring it into subjection: lest that by any means, when I have preached to others, I myself should be a castaway." He feared that if he did not keep down this old carnal nature, keep it under subjection, that he who had been so greatly used in preaching the gospel might fall into grievous sin and be laid on the shelf so God could use him no more in soul winning.

I am sorry that David did not take into account that old wicked nature within him. And let all of us remember that we have the same kind of a nature.

Do you remember the story of how one Greek city warred against another, and the besiegers left a giant wooden horse with some soldiers concealed inside? When the besiegers withdrew, then the men of the city dragged the wooden horse inside, and rejoiced at their capture. But when night was come, the soldiers hidden inside got out of the wooden horse and opened the gates of the city to the invading army.

Oh, a Christian might resist all the wiles of the enemy, as

long as the enemy is on the outside. But the sad truth is that every Christian has a traitor within his own body. He has longings, desires, and temptations that flow from his own unsanctified human nature. The first child ever born in this world turned out to be Cain, a murderer; and every child born since is tainted by nature, alien from God, with an innate tendency to evil. How watchful, how prayerful one should be, how circumspect in the effort to buffet the carnal nature and keep the bodily nature in subjection lest one should fall into sin! David was dragged into sin by his own innate nature, as he himself later admitted in Psalm 51:5.

Jesus warned the boastful Peter: "Watch and pray, that ye enter not into temptation: the spirit indeed is willing, but the flesh is weak" (Matt. 26:41). But Peter did not listen to the warning and so fell into terrible temptation, denied the Saviour, cursed and swore, then quit the ministry! Oh, let us watch and pray, lest we fall into temptation because of our weak flesh!

III. The Progress of Hidden Sin

No tragedy of Shakespeare is as tragic as the tragedy of David's sin. Consider for a bit how sin grew and flourished when it was not instantly repudiated, or when it was not confessed at once and forsaken.

First, David enjoyed his desire and encouraged it. But after dallying with temptation it became soon too strong for him to resist.

David's temptation was like the boa constrictor, the giant snake which a man raised from babyhood until it was eighteen feet long. It would coil itself about him in play and release him at a command. The man made much money by having the great reptile coil about his body on the stage. The snake could have killed a deer or an ox by constricting its muscles, but the man was accustomed to it and the snake obeyed his commands. But one day the snake was angry; and when he gave the command to release him, instead it crushed him to death in a moment. So when we play with temptation, we are enslaved by it and killed by it.

A little vine grows about a big tree and one thinks nothing of it. But eventually the vine becomes strong and saps the life of the tree and the tree dies. The gaunt trunk of the dead tree becomes simply the trellis for the overmastering parasite. So a man plays with temptation and then is mastered by it.

Can you imagine the mixed emotions, the struggle of soul that went on in the heart of David? David was a loyal friend. Do you remember how he loved Jonathan? Do you remember how he cared for Mephibosheth? Do you remember his loyalty to Barzillai the Gileadite, who fed him and cared for him when he fled Absalom? David was a tender man, a loyal man. He must have thought much and perhaps was tormented at the thought of wronging Uriah, one of his devoted and valiant bodyguard. But soon David had gone too far and he threw his fears to the wind. For the moment he was overwhelmed with his own passion. He committed the deadly sin. He stole the affection of his friend's wife and led her into adultery. It was a terrible sin. According to the Mosaic law in Leviticus 20:10, it deserved death. And that idleness and foolish sense of his kingly importance which would not allow him to be brought before a court of justice, and his dallying with his sin, and his own carnal nature, led David over the brink into this shameful sin.

I suppose there were days of fear and trembling, days of humiliation of heart, days of shamed conscience after his sin with Bath-sheba. I warn you now, dear Christian, that you may sin with little thought of the future, but as certain as you are a child of God, you will be made miserable for your sin. The man or woman who can go into sin and not be troubled about it later must surely never have been born again.

Then one day David's greatest fears were confirmed. A message came from Bath-sheba. "I am with child," she said.

His greatest fears are realized. His sin is about to be brought to public exposure. What will David do?

You may be sure there was more heart-searching, then David planned what to do. He would send for Uriah, have him spend some days at home. Then when the baby was born no one could accuse David.

But Uriah, when brought from the battle, could not feel content to enjoy his home. His mind was on the place of duty. He was a valiant and loyal soldier. Joab, the army general, was still in the field of war. All his companions who had vied with him in doing mighty exploits were camped in the open field and in tents. So Uriah slept at the door of the king's house and was ready when the early morning came to return to the battle.

This time David thought to make Uriah drunk and felt that surely drink would drown the patriotism that burned so warmly in Uriah's heart. But a second time, even when David had made him drunk, Uriah slept on his pallet nearby and did not go down to his house, did not see his wife.

David was desperate. He felt he must avoid a scandal at all costs. He suffered more fear because he was really, genuinely, a spiritual man. The sin seemed more horrible to him than it would to one who went regularly into such terrible God-dishonoring practices. At all costs, David felt, he must keep his sin hidden. So now, as a last resort, he planned to have Uriah killed. He wrote a letter to Joab and sent it by the hand of Uriah. Perhaps Uriah could not read. If he could read, such a loyal man would never think of opening a letter entrusted to him for another. So the loyal, good soldier left David, with words of love and admiration, and went out to the battle, not knowing that the man he loved had sent him to his death. The man he trusted was his murderer!

Joab, receiving David's instructions, put Uriah in the forefront of the battle, and Uriah was killed by the men of the besieged city. In the words of Nathan the prophet, David killed Uriah "with the sword of the children of Ammon"

(II Sam. 12:9). A man who was first careless in his prayer life and ignored his carnal nature and the temptations of the flesh, has now been led into the worst possible sin. The man who dallied with temptation and looked on another man's wife and led her into adultery has now become a murderer!

Hear me! If you begin the road of sin you will come out at a destination you never expected! I have talked with many a criminal. I say "criminals," but actually they were ordinary people, very little different from you and me. And again and again the man or woman who was an embezzler, or a murderer, has said to me, "Whatever possessed me to commit such a sin! I never dreamed I would do a thing like that!" You see, the harlot never intended to become a harlot when she first went to the dance or when she allowed promiscuous necking and petting. You see, the man never intended to be a whoremonger when he looked at a woman to lust after her. You see, a murderer never intended to be a murderer when he first allowed hate to find lodgment in his heart. Sin may have small beginnings but it has fearful endings! Lust may seem a long way from murder but in James 1:15 we are told: "Then when lust hath conceived, it bringeth forth sin: and sin, when it is finished, bringeth forth death."

Dr. T. DeWitt Talmage well has said,

> "Sin may open bright as the morning, but it will end dark as the night."

David found it so!

Again, let Dr. Bob Jones, Sr., the mighty evangelist, provide us an illustration. Dr. Jones said in my hearing that he read with astonishment in a daily paper that a certain pastor was accused of murdering the woman choir leader in his church. Dr. Jones said to a friend, "That is a lie! That preacher never did anything of the kind! He is one of the purest, best men I ever saw. I have preached in his church. I have been in his home. He is a good man. He might make minor mistakes but he is not a murderer. I know he did not kill that woman as the newspaper reports indicate."

But Dr. Bob tells us that the next day the newspapers carried the confession, signed by the preacher. He had fallen in love with the choir singer. They had carried on an affair long years. At last when exposure was threatened and the man's entire ministry was at stake, he killed her. He did that which he never dreamed he would do. Sin had a different ending to what he expected. And so it always is with sin.

An old proverb says:

> "Oh, what a tangled web we weave
> When first we practice to deceive."

One sin leads to another. And I will tell you now, that there is only one remedy that can stop the growing floodtide of sin when it starts in the heart. There is only one way that one may break the chords that are beginning to bind and enslave a man or woman in sin. And that one remedy is confession to God, in honest repentance. As long as one covers his sin and tries to hide it, he will go further in sin. As long as one excuses his sin and has an alibi for it, and hugs the sin to his bosom, he will commit more sin and go on in his enslavement. But, thank God, when a man turns to God in honest, heartbroken confession and admits his sin and comes for the mercy that is promised to the penitent sinner, then the enchantment that ensnares him is broken. The enslaving passion is cleansed.

Oh, if we but knew it, the sin of all sins is to hide sin in the heart, to make excuses for it, to dally with it and temporize with it! The appeasement of Chamberlain and others did not work with Hitler. The appeasement of President Roosevelt at Yalta and Potsdam and of Truman later did not work with Stalin and atheistic, communistic Russia. So the appeasement of sin never does work out well. It always leads to further enslavement and ruin.

I studied most carefully the career of one great criminal in Texas who for murders and every kind of crime was finally assessed total penalties of some four hundred years in the penitentiary before he was at last given the death penalty for another murder. Do you know how he started? He started by first stealing chickens, and then stealing tires and batteries off of cars! Hardly anybody believes that stealing watermelons or chickens is the way to murder and the electric chair. But it is! And hardly any Christian will believe that promiscuous necking and the dance and nude pictures are the way to adultery and murder. But they are! Oh, sin, unconfessed sin, sin that is hidden in the heart, sin that is appeased and temporized with—such sin leads to utter ruin. So it did, even with the godly man, David, the anointed king, the Spirit-filled prophet. And so it will with you, whoever you be, who temporize with sin, coddle it, do not confess it, and forsake it.

IV. The Sin Exposed

Now we must read more of the story in the Scripture and find what followed the terrible sin. Second Samuel 12:1–14 tells of how Nathan the prophet came to David and boldly accused him of his sin.

"And the Lord sent Nathan unto David. And he came unto him, and said unto him, There were two men in one city; the one rich, and the other poor. The rich man had exceeding many flocks and herds: But the poor man had nothing, save one little ewe lamb, which he had bought and nourished up: and it grew up together with him, and with his children; it did eat of his own meat, and drank of his own cup, and lay in his bosom, and was unto him as a daughter. And there came a traveller unto the rich man, and he spared to take of his own flock and of his own herd, to dress for the wayfaring man that was come unto him; but took the poor man's lamb, and dressed it for the man that was come to him. And David's anger was greatly kindled against the man; and he said to Nathan, As the Lord liveth, the man that hath done this thing shall surely die. And he shall restore the lamb fourfold, because he did this thing, and because he had no pity. And Nathan said to David, Thou art the man. Thus saith the

Lord God of Israel, I anointed thee king over Israel, and I delivered thee out of the hand of Saul; And I gave thee thy master's house, and thy master's wives into thy bosom, and gave thee the house of Israel and of Judah; and if that had been too little, I would moreover have given unto thee such and such things. Wherefore hast thou despised the commandment of the Lord, to do evil in his sight? thou hast killed Uriah the Hittite with the sword, and hast taken his wife to be thy wife, and hast slain him with the sword of the children of Ammon. Now therefore the sword shall never depart from thine house; because thou hast despised me, and hast taken the wife of Uriah the Hittite to be thy wife. Thus saith the Lord, Behold, I will raise up evil against thee out of thine own house, and I will take thy wives before thine eyes, and give them unto thy neighbour, and he shall lie with thy wives in the sight of this sun. For thou didst it secretly: but I will do this thing before all Israel, and before the sun. And David said unto Nathan, I have sinned against the Lord. And Nathan said unto David, The Lord also hath put away thy sin; thou shalt not die. Howbeit, because by this deed thou hast given great occasion to the enemies of the Lord to blaspheme, the child also that is born unto thee shall surely die."
—II Sam. 12:1–14.

Thank God for faithful Nathan, the prophet! He received a message from God and delivered it to David. David could have killed him for it. Other kings did kill faithful prophets for the same kind of word from God.

Nathan was somewhat like John the Baptist who came face to face with King Herod and said, "It is not lawful for thee to have thy brother's wife." And from that moment Herodias, the adulterous wife, hated John the Baptist and determined to have him killed. Eventually, when her daughter danced before Herod and was promised whatever she would ask, she was taught by Herodias to ask for the head of John the Baptist in a charger. John the Baptist, saint of God, forerunner of the Saviour, the equal of any prophet ever born, was killed because he told a king the truth about his sins.

But in some ways Nathan's task was even more difficult. Nathan loved David. David was a good man. David was a prophet of God. David had been inspired to write Psalms for the Word of God. David had been given the honor of becoming the ancestor of Jesus Christ and the founder of the throne on which Christ will one day reign. How hard it must have been for Nathan to face David! It is not difficult for a Southern Baptist preacher to show the sins of Catholics. But it would be very difficult for a loyal Southern Baptist preacher to expose modernism in the Southern Baptist Seminary at Louisville. It would not be so difficult for an independent Fundamentalist Christian man to expose the National Council of Churches. But how hard it would be for him to expose a bad book published by his favorite Bible institute or Christian college and endorsed by leading fundamentalists! It is harder for a pastor to oppose the sin which goes on among his own members who love him and support him than it would be to preach on the sins of New York society! Nathan had a difficult job. O God, raise up more Nathans! May God give more ministers who can stand for God against a denominational bishop, a king, or a friend. Nathan faced King David whom he loved and revered and told him about his sin.

It is a charming and pathetic story which Nathan told. A rich man with many flocks and herds stole the one little ewe lamb, the pet and joy of the poor man, and that little ewe lamb was prepared and served in style to company of the rich man.

Was Nathan referring to David's own sin? David thought not. How would Nathan know about it? The pieces of the puzzle were scattered so that no one could possibly know the whole story. A servant of David would know about the adultery, and Joab would know about the death of Uriah, but no one would know all the facts. I imagine it did not enter David's mind that Nathan referred to him. But God had revealed it to Nathan.

David's anger was so kindled that he pronounced judgment on the wicked man who had so sinned against his neighbor. First, the man should surely die; and, second, he should restore the lamb fourfold. And then Nathan plainly said, "Thou art the man."

Never had a man been more blessed than David. God had showered upon him blessings. He had given him the kingdom, had given him wives, had given him servants, had given him riches. If he had wanted or needed more, God would have given them. But David had wickedly taken a poor man's wife, his joy and delight, and had committed adultery with the wife of a friend who trusted him, then had murdered his friend! We can hardly think of a more terrible crime. And now the sin is out. God brings sin to light.

Do you think that your sin is hidden away? Do you think that men will never know it? Well, you should remember that God knows it already. And you should remember, second, that sin continued in will inevitably come to light. Usually it will be exposed in this life. Certainly it will be exposed when you stand before God and God's record books are opened. That which is whispered in a corner shall be shouted from the housetop. God will bring every secret thing to judgment, we are told. What warning to our hearts! Oh, believe me, dear reader! You cannot get by with sin. Even if you are a king, you cannot get by. Even if no one knows it, you cannot get by! God will bring sin to judgment. "Be sure your sin will find you out."

V. The Fourfold Reaping of Sin

We must remember that David, though he has sinned, is the prophet of God. Although he has followed on from one terrible sin to another, we must not believe that he loves sin or that he has given himself up to sin. David is God's man, a born-again Christian. David wants to do right. He has been overwhelmed with temptation, but he is still God's man. And so when Nathan tells him the story of a wicked man who has oppressed his neighbor and stolen the one ewe lamb, David, as a prophet of God, gives proper judgment. The man deserves death. The lamb must be restored fourfold.

David did not know it, but he was pronouncing judgment upon himself. He was to suffer and to pay four terrible times for the sin of his adultery and murder.

First, we are told, "And Nathan departed unto his house. And the Lord struck the child that Uriah's wife bare unto David, and it was very sick." The child must die. That is payment number one of the account.

Oh, how David besought the Lord for the child! David fasted and lay all night on the earth. We know that his heart was penitent. We know that he pleaded for God's mercy. But the child that was stricken died.

The servants feared to tell David that the child was dead. They thought that surely now David would be almost deranged with grief. But David seems to have thought in his heart, "Perhaps the worst is over. God in His mercy has punished me, but I deserved it. Perhaps this is the end of the matter." So David comforted Bath-sheba and God in His mercy gave to David and Bath-sheba a second son, Solomon.

We dare to think that this child was given in answer to prayer. He was loved of God and God chose him to be David's successor and to sit on David's throne, though he was not the elder son. And Solomon was so blessed of God that we must not believe that any curse remained on him because of his father's and mother's sin. And yet the debt is not fully paid. "Fourfold," David the prophet had said. Now David the sinner must pay.

The next chapter tells us of Amnon's crime. Amnon was the spoiled son of David, and he fell in love with his half sister, Tamar. Nothing would do but that Tamar must come to his apartment and cook for him, and there the innocent girl was ravished. She went away weeping, and Absalom, her full brother, saw her, inquired where she had been, and took her to his home.

Poor David! Can anyone imagine the shame and grief of his heart when he learned that his beautiful daughter, Tamar, had been ruined by her own brother, David's son? Can you imagine the accusings of his conscience? Can you imagine how he blamed himself: "How can I punish the boy? He has sinned as I sinned! I am reaping what I have sown!" Yet I imagine that after David's great trouble of heart and smitings of conscience he may have comforted himself and thought that the debt was paid in full. But, David, you must still reap the rest of the fourfold punishment that as the prophet of God you pronounced upon yourself so unsuspectingly.

Absalom, Tamar's brother, hated his half-brother, Amnon, and determined to kill him. He made a feast for the king's sons and then instructed his servants: "Mark you now when Amnon's heart is merry with wine, and when I say unto you, Smite Amnon; then kill him, fear not: have not I commanded you? Be courageous, and be valiant." So when the party was on and Amnon had been drinking, Absalom commanded his servants and they killed the young man who had raped Absalom's sister, Tamar. And all the other king's sons fled the home to Jerusalem. But Absalom ran away to Talmai, the son of Ammihud, king of Geshur (II Sam. 13:37). It seems that that was the home of his mother, David's wife, Maachah, daughter of the king of Geshur. And we are told sadly, "And David mourned for his son every day."

O David, David! Grieving over a ruined daughter, and now grieving over a murdered son! Is the debt all paid, David? Do you think that is the end of your sin? I wonder if David pondered the matter and thought that at long last he had outlived the results of his sin? But he had not. He had said, "And he shall restore the lamb fourfold" (II Sam. 12:6) and you have yet a payment to make for your sin, dear David.

The fourteenth and fifteenth chapters of II Samuel tell how Absalom was brought back to Jerusalem and partly forgiven and then how Absalom stole away the hearts of the people, rebelled against King David, and how David ran for his life from the city.

Can you imagine the despair of heart of King David as he flees from his own son, driven from his throne and palace and capital city by a rebel mob? And Shimei followed and threw stones at David, and called him a bloody man. This was a disgrace almost too much to bear and Abishai, loyal nephew of David, turned to the king and said, "Why should this dead dog curse my lord the king? Let me go I pray thee and take off his head?" But the king sadly turned to this young man and said, "So let him curse, because the Lord hath said unto him, Curse David. Who shall then say, Wherefore hast thou done so?" (II Sam. 16:10).

You know the rest of the story, how David hid out in dens and caves, how the friends of David assembled against the armies led by Absalom in a mighty battle. You know how Absalom's head was caught in the branches of an oak tree, and there they found him and shot him through with darts, and Absalom died.

King David had said to Joab when he went out that morning to the battle, "Deal gently with the young man Absalom." But when the messenger came to bring David news of the battle and David asked about Absalom, the messenger said, "May all the enemies of my lord the king be as that young man is this day." And David turned and went up into the room over the city gate, and wept as he went. And thus he said, "O my son Absalom, my son, my son Absalom! Would God I had died for thee, O Absalom, my son, my son!" (II Sam. 18:33). David has paid in full the heavy price, the fourfold price for his sin.

David knows now that they that sow to the wind shall reap the whirlwind. David knows now that sin brings forth an increased crop.

Years ago a wicked, drunken old man was saved at Evansville, Indiana. They called him "Old Bill." He had had an eye put out in a drunken fight. Then he was wonderfully saved.

He called himself now "New Bill" because God had made him new. He gave his testimony far and near as to what God would do for a poor ruined sinner who would trust him. But to his dying day New Bill still had only one eye. He found that though his sin was forgiven, he must pay. And so it is with a Christian who goes into sin. He may be forgiven, but he must still pay on his debt. I pray that God may let it sink solemnly into my heart and into yours that sin is a dreadful, hateful, fearsome business; that the wages of sin are bitter, bitter beyond any human computation! I pray that every Christian may so watch and pray with fear and trembling that he may be spared from such terrible sins as David's, for you may be sure that your sins will find you out!

VI. Sin Gloriously Put Away and Forgiven!

I could not leave this heart-rending story without telling you the wonderful truth of God's cleansing and forgiveness. David did commit a terrible sin, and he suffered for it. But, thank God, his sin was forgiven and covered. And David received sweet peace, and God did not withdraw His Spirit from David. David received again the sweet joy of his salvation.

First, let us consider the penitent prayer of David.

The traditional note above Psalm 51 is as follows: "To the chief Musician, A Psalm of David, when Nathan the prophet came unto him, after he had gone in to Bath-sheba." That explanatory note does not claim to be a part of the Bible, and yet we believe it is correct. The fifty-first Psalm is the penitential prayer of David after his sin had been forcibly brought to his mind by Nathan the prophet.

Let us read that penitential Psalm 51 as the heart-cry of a Christian who has done wrong.

"Have mercy upon me, O God, according to thy loving-kindness: according unto the multitude of thy tender mercies blot out my transgressions. Wash me throughly from mine

iniquity, and cleanse me from my sin. For I acknowledge my transgressions: and my sin is ever before me. Against thee, thee only, have I sinned, and done this evil in thy sight: that thou mightest be justified when thou speakest, and be clear when thou judgest. Behold, I was shapen in iniquity; and in sin did my mother conceive me. Behold, thou desirest truth in the inward parts: and in the hidden part thou shalt make me to know wisdom. Purge me with hyssop, and I shall be clean: wash me, and I shall be whiter than snow. Make me to hear joy and gladness; that the bones which thou hast broken may rejoice. Hide thy face from my sins, and blot out all mine iniquities. Create in me a clean heart, O God; and renew a right spirit within me. Cast me not away from thy presence; and take not thy holy spirit from me. Restore unto me the joy of thy salvation; and uphold me with thy free spirit. Then will I teach transgressors thy ways; and sinners shall be converted unto thee. Deliver me from bloodguiltiness, O God, thou God of my salvation: and my tongue shall sing aloud of thy righteousness. O Lord, open thou my lips; and my mouth shall shew forth thy praise. For thou desirest not sacrifice; else would I give it: thou delightest not in burnt-offering. The sacrifices of God are a broken spirit: a broken and a contrite heart, O God, thou wilt not despise. Do good in thy good pleasure unto Zion: build thou the walls of Jerusalem. Then shalt thou be pleased with the sacrifices of righteousness, with burnt-offering and whole burnt-offering: then shall they offer bullocks upon thine altar."

I have not time to preach on this wonderful Psalm. Second Samuel 12:20 tells us that after David's baby died he washed and anointed himself and changed his apparel and came into the house of the Lord and worshiped. It may be that then he wrote this wonderful Psalm. Or it may be that in those days of fasting and prayer while the baby was stricken and before it died that David wrote these pleading words of prayer. I do not know. But we should notice that David here thoroughly confesses his sin, confesses his weakness, admits his guilt before God. He pleads for cleansing. He pleads that God will hide his face from sin, will make David's spirit right. He pleads that God will not cast him away from conscious fellowship with Him and that God will not take the Holy Spirit from him. We know that this prayer was answered. David prayed that God would restore to him the joy of salvation and uphold him. "Then," said David, "will I teach transgressors thy ways; and sinners shall be converted unto thee. Deliver me from bloodguiltiness, O God, thou God of my salvation: and my tongue shall sing aloud of thy righteousness." Oh, even in that time when he is conscious of his sin, David is pleading that he may still be made fit to be a soul winner. And he offers to God the one sacrifice that God wants from a sinner—a broken and contrite heart. Such an offering God will never despise.

So David was restored to fellowship and restored to joy. God still wonderfully used him as He had done before.

But we have neglected a brief word or two in the story, which I wish now to call to your attention. When Nathan the prophet had told David of the rich man who stole the poor man's lamb, David said, "As the Lord liveth, the man that hath done this thing shall surely die." Then David said that the lamb should be restored fourfold. It is a striking thing that David had to fulfill the prophecy about the fourfold payment of the lamb. David lost his baby, then had his daughter raped, then had his son assassinated by Absalom, then had Absalom to rebel, to commit fornication with David's own concubines on the housetop, and then die in rebellion against David. But while the prophecy in verse 6 was fulfilled, the prophecy in verse 5 was not. David did not die for this sin. Second Samuel 12:13 tells us: "And David said unto Nathan, I have sinned against the Lord. And Nathan said unto David, The Lord also hath put away thy sin; thou shalt not die." David's sin was put away. David did not die.

And this for us pictures the wonderful truth of salvation. Every one who was ever saved was a lost sinner condemned to die, who deserved to die, not only death in the flesh but death in the spirit. Every sinner ever saved deserved not only the first death but also the second death. But those who come and put their trust in Jesus, as David had done, have their sins put away, have their sins forgiven, have everlasting life instead of death.

That term "put away" which God uses about David's sin is a beautiful term. That is the term used in Hebrews 9:26 about Jesus: ". . . but now once in the end of the world hath he appeared to put away sin by the sacrifice of himself." And the two following verses say, "And as it is appointed unto men once to die, but after this the judgment: so Christ was once offered to bear the sins of many; and unto them that look for him shall he appear the second time without sin unto salvation."

Oh, glorious truth that Christ has appeared and taketh away sin by the sacrifice of Himself! The reason David did not die is because he had trusted the coming Messiah to pay for his sins. God offered Jesus to put away sin by the sacrifice of Himself. Now, although it is appointed for all of us to die, and every man and woman who was ever born deserves to die in his sins and go to Hell, yet, thank God, Christ, offered for our sins once, is coming again. And when He comes, "shall he appear the second time without sin unto salvation." That is, the sins of ours will not appear. Christ has already borne them, put them away, paid for them. And when we see Jesus He will not reproach us with them, because they are under the blood and we do not have to die the eternal death.

The dear Lord Jesus died in my place. That is the only hope I have of salvation! He died to put away my sin. That is the only hope I have of missing Hell. Jesus offered Himself as a sacrifice to put away sin. And my sins, thank God, are put away!

I know no other assurance in this world as precious as this assurance that one's sin is paid for and put away.

You remember that Isaiah 44:22 says, "I have blotted out, as a thick cloud, thy transgressions, and, as a cloud, thy sins: return unto me; for I have redeemed thee." That is not for Jews alone, it is for me, and for everybody else who will trust in the shed blood of Jesus Christ, who came to put away sin by the sacrifice of Himself. Every one who comes to Jesus Christ has his sins put away. One who comes to Christ has his sins blotted out. One who comes to Christ has his sins carried as far as the east is from the west, an infinite distance, for Psalm 103:12 says, "As far as the east is from the west, so far hath he removed our transgressions from us." And Hebrews 10:17 tells us, "And their sins and iniquities will I remember no more." Thank God, when He forgives a sinner's sin, they are put away forever so that even God forgets them, and will not remember them.

There are two solemn invitations which I want to put in writing here at the end of this sermon on "David and Bathsheba." One is for those who are Christians, but who know they have gone into sin, know there is sin in their lives, know that they have grieved God, know they have covered up sin in their lives, and so are subject to God's angry judgments. If you know that you have sinned against God, you need not tell me what it was. Won't you confess it to God now, honestly uncover the matter in your heart? Face it, and confess it, renounce it and with all your heart penitently turn from it today, and ask God to blot it out forever! If there is a sin against somebody else that you ought to make right, then do it today. If there is a debt unpaid, go pay it. If there is something stolen to be restored, then restore it, with interest. If you owe an apology, go make it. If there is wrong unrighted, in Jesus' name, go make it right today. If there is a brother estranged, offended, then go and apologize. Remember that Jesus said, "Therefore if thou bring thy gift to the altar, and there rememberest that thy brother hath ought against thee; Leave there thy gift before the altar, and go thy way; first be reconciled to thy brother, and then come and offer thy gift" (Matt. 5:23, 24). Oh, be reconciled today with anyone with whom you are at variance! Forgive and be forgiven. Throw away your grudges against others, and go in tender humility to beg forgiveness of any who have grudges against you!

I say, the first invitation is to Christians. If you will honestly confess to God some serious sin, and honestly turn away from that sin, and make whatever restitution is possible or necessary, as God gives you grace, then sign the decision form, or copy it in a letter, and send it to me. Let that be a token between you and God that you are honestly facing your sin with Him and will do your utmost to make it right.

Decision for Sinning Christians

Evangelist John R. Rice
The Sword of the Lord
Murfreesboro, Tennessee 37130

DEAR BROTHER RICE:

I have read your sermon on "David and Bath-sheba." God has brought to mind a matter in which I have seriously sinned against Him, but had not yet confessed it to Him, nor honestly faced it. I here and now confess my sin to God. I will ask Him to cleanse me and forgive me. I will ask Him to show me how I may make it right with others. And as God leads I will make whatever restitution seems necessary or possible, and set out to make sure that the sin is cleansed out of my life. I confess it to God and claim His promise of cleansing and forgiveness, according to I John 1:9. I trust Him to restore the joy of my salvation and help me to win souls and live in His joy and power.

Signed ____

Address ____

____

Decision for Lost Sinners

But some sinner has read this who knows himself to be an unconverted, unforgiven sinner. Oh, sinner, how will you face the God of judgment, the God who punishes His own dear saints, who punished David, a man so dear to God? How will you expect to get by with your sin when you have not repented, when you have not trusted Christ for forgiveness? In Jesus' dear name I beg you today to repent of your sins and trust Christ for forgiveness.

He loves you. If you will depend upon Him this moment, He will forgive you. I beg you to trust Him now, this very moment, with all your heart. Confess your sin and believe that He forgives you, because He died for you and because He has promised. "Believe on the Lord Jesus Christ, and thou shalt be saved," is the plain promise of Acts 16:31. Will you trust today and with penitent heart receive His forgiveness? If you will, won't you sign the decision form here, then copy it on a letter or card and mail it to me at once? Say yes in your heart to God, and receive His forgiveness. I will be so glad to hear that you are trusting the Saviour. I will write you a letter of encouragement and counsel. Will you here and now turn away from your sins and give your heart to Jesus Christ forever? If you will, then say yes in your heart, sign the decision form, copy it and mail it at once.

Evanglist John R. Rice
The Sword of the Lord
Murfreesboro, Tennessee 37130

DEAR BROTHER RICE:

I have read your sermon on "David and Bath-sheba." I feel moved in my heart to confess that I am a poor lost sinner. I want God to forgive me and save me. I believe that Jesus died for me. I believe that He is willing to put away my sins and forgive them as He promised to do for those who trust Him.

Here and now, with all my heart I trust Christ to forgive my sins, I depend upon Him to save my soul. This moment I take Him as my own Saviour. By His grace I will confess Him before men and set out to live for Him the balance of my life.

Signed ______________________________

Address ______________________________

____